HAWAI'I GEOGRAPHIC PUBLICATIONS
Order Desk: USA
Hawai'i/Worldwide ¬   808-538-3952
Honolulu, HAWAI'I   96806-1698

HAWAIIAN
HIKING TRAILS

Craig Chisholm

Revised and Updated Edition

The Fernglen Press
473 Sixth Street
Lake Oswego, Oregon 97034

Maps: Courtesy of U.S. Geological Survey
Design: Corinna Campbell
Printed in the United States of America

Library of Congress Cataloging in Publication Data
Chisholm, Craig M.
Hawaiian Hiking Trails
Revised and Updated Edition
Seventh Edition
152 p. : maps, drawings, and photos (some color)
1. Hiking — Hawaii — Guide-books
2. Trails — Hawaii — Guide-books
3. Hawaiian Islands — Description and travel — 1981-
   — Guide-books
I. Title
GV199.42.H3 C47 1989 919.69/044 89-83996
ISBN 0-9612630-2-4

Na Pali Coast—Kauai

Halemauu Trail—Haleakala Crater, Maui

Silversword and evening primrose—Haleakala Crater

Pahoehoe lava—Hawaii Volcanoes National Park

Spring on Mauna Loa

Ohia lehua blossoms

Ohelo berries

Cinder cone—devastation and regeneration

Tree molds—Mauna Loa in the background   *Akaka Falls—Hawaii*

Ohia and fern forest—Kilauea Iki Trail   *Near Akaka Falls*

Sunset at Pu'uhonua-o-Honaunau

Polihua Beach—Lanai

Along the road to Polihua Beach—Molokai in the background

Amaumau fern (sadleria) along Halemauu Trail, Maui

Amaumau fiddlehead

Young amaumau fern (sadleria)

Lace fern (sphenomeris chusana)

Swordfern

Kalaupapa Peninsula — a classic shield volcano

Waimea Canyon—Kauai

Hanakapiai Falls — Kauai

In memory of
Dr. Douglas Murray Burns
Wise teacher and friend of my youth

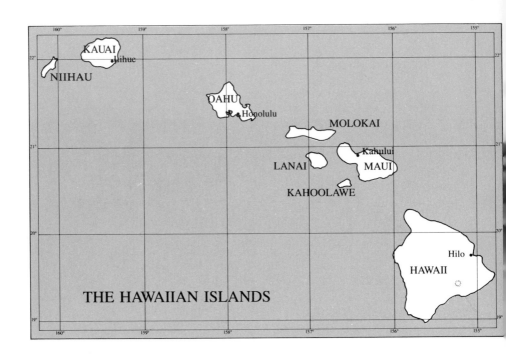

THE HAWAIIAN ISLANDS

Contents

Acknowledgments

I am greatly indebted to the many people who have helped on this book. Among them I would particularly like to acknowledge the assistance of the following: The personnel of the National Park Service and the Hawaii State Department of Land and Natural Resources who have been most generous and thoughtful in providing information and answering questions; Scholastica Murty, Marian Wood, John Hedlund, Henry Richmond, and Steve and Carol Pinnell for their careful readings of the manuscript; Dr. T. Hayden Gill for his advice on calorie consumption; Dr. Buz Willett, the Nishimura family, and the personnel of the Lanai Company for their warm hospitality and help on the Island of Lanai; Sandra Stallcup for her work on Akaka Trail; the members of the Hawaiian Trail and Mountain Club and the Sierra Club who shared their experiences and were most helpful in their advice; John and Sinikka Hayasaka for their encouragement; my family for their patience and help, especially my father, Colin Chisholm, who taught me early a love for the hills.

Editor
Eila Chisholm

Photography by Craig Chisholm
Colin Chisholm, p. 8, upper left
Eila Chisholm, pp. 7, 10, and 83
Nicki Clancey, pp. 120 and 121
Jeff Dunn, p. 39
Ellen Schroeder, pp. 103 and 113
Sandra Stallcup, p. 49
Herbert Warner, p. 109

Drawings
Ellen Schroeder

Preface to Revised and Updated Edition

Hawaii's landscape changes rapidly. Trails are obliterated by erosion and encroaching vegetation, submerged by earthquakes and tidal waves, covered by lava, added to, or changed for a variety of administrative reasons. Even the type of vegetation in many areas is changing, with endemic plants disappearing in the face of aggressive, common new varieties.

This edition has been revised and updated to incorporate the numerous changes since the book was first published. Most of the maps have been redrawn or amended, many of the black and white photos have been improved upon, and a color section has been added in order to give the reader a more complete view of the scenery. This considerable effort would not have been accomplished without the able assistance and gentle encouragement of my wife, Eila.

The various agencies administering the lands have continued to generously provide valuable information and advice. In particular, I wish to thank Dr. Mona Bomgaars, Wayne Ching, Barry Cooper, Ralph Daehler, Jon Erickson, Riki Hokama, Galen Kawakami, Herbert Kikukawa, Dennis Knuckles, Ralston Nagata, Ernest Pung, and Jerry Shimoda.

Craig Chisholm
Lake Oswego, Oregon

Introduction

Many lament the ruin of what once made Hawaii an earthly paradise. Memories are evoked of uncrowded valleys and seashores, now cluttered with highrise dwellings, highways, crowds, and commercialism. Fortunately, this is true only for those who refuse to leave the comfort of their cars. The best of Hawaii still awaits those willing to walk: isolated black-sand beaches, waterfalls cascading into clear pools, valleys dotted with stone ruins, groves of fruit trees planted by long-vanished people, and mountain regions of spectacular beauty.

Many hiking trails lead to these quiet scenes. This book covers a wide selection of the best, described in enough detail to allow the reader to choose suitable trails and areas. The trails included range from pleasant strolls to memorable "character builders." Some fine trails are not described here because of access problems. Too little has been done to assure access to public lands. Hopefully, well-considered planning will improve hiking access to the back country as well as preserve the rights of private landowners.

Climate and Topography

The weather in the Hawaiian Islands varies dramatically from one area to the next but it is remarkably stable the year round in any one place. The constant tradewinds out of the northeast, passing over the rugged terrain, create distinct, almost invariable lines between microclimates. The vastness of the Pacific Ocean moderates the temperature of these trade winds and minimizes seasonal change. The occasional warm, humid Kona winds from the south only occasionally vary this pattern. As the trade winds rise over the mountainous islands, they cool to form clouds which release their moisture, mostly between 3,000 and 7,000 feet. Higher and lower elevations receive progressively less moisture. The wettest months are between October and April.

The islands were formed by shield volcanoes rising slowly from the ocean floor to form gently sloping, symmetrical mountains. Today's rugged peaks and valleys were shaped by millennia of erosion that faithfully reflect the invariable weather patterns.

Erosion is increasingly evident proceeding northwest from the gentle slopes of the young island of Hawaii to the ancient and precipitous Na Pali Coast of Kauai. Generally, the deepest valleys begin where rainfall is heaviest, on the north or northeast sides of each island. The highest sea cliffs and most rugged coastlines are usually on the north coasts, where wave action is strongest.

Clothing and Equipment

A pleasant part of hiking in Hawaii is that relatively little equipment is needed. However, this is *not* true of the hikes on Haleakala and Mauna Loa which require equipment comparable to that used for mountain climbing on the mainland, such as, tents, heavy wool clothing, and rain gear. The temperature drops 3 to 5 degrees Fahrenheit for every 1,000 feet gained in elevation. Hikes into the wet areas above 2,000 feet can be unpleasant and dangerous, if the traveler becomes wet or is overtaken by darkness. Waterproof and wool clothing should be carried, the latter because it retains some warmth even when wet. Exposure has been a complication in many rescues.

Stout, broken-in boots are needed for hikes on the high mountains or over rough lava; tennis shoes are fine for short hikes. Long pants are the rule because of heavy brush along the trails. Sunglasses are desirable near the sea and goggles are mandatory in the high, snow-covered mountains. Many visitors from the mainland can receive painful sunburns and therefore should use protective lotion. Rain gear near sea level is optional; some prefer to hike in light clothing, get wet in the warm rain, and dry out later. After all, one can only get so wet. Tents may be required for camping in some areas. They are necessary at high elevations, and may be of value in keeping out insects and rain. Plastic ground covers can double as ponchos and picnic cloths. Insect repellent, flashlights, and a compass are useful. Usually only light sleeping bags are needed. Unfortunately, frame packs may not be allowed on buses.

Plants and Animals

The isolation of the Hawaiian Islands allowed the evolution of life forms fascinatingly different from those found in continental regions. In prehistoric times, plants and animals traveled great distances from their original homes to flourish in the islands, free from their natural enemies. In time, these original species evolved into new life forms found nowhere else, filling the various ecological niches in these islands.

The pigs, dogs, rats, and fire brought by the original Polynesians began the process of ecological damage. The original plants and animals suffered even more grievously when they came into contact with the rest of the world. These gentle life forms, no longer protected by thorns, poisons, deep roots, vigorous regenerative powers, and resistance to disease, could not compete successfully against the hardy, newly imported life forms. Foreign diseases, carelessly introduced species of plants and insects, voracious livestock, and wild fire have destroyed vast portions of the original flora, and have led to the extermination of whole species of desirable plants and ani-mals. No other state's life forms have seen and continue to see such a thorough destruction. Domestic and wild livestock were steadily destroying the forested areas on all the islands until the early part of this century. When the water supplies became imperiled, the government set aside forest areas for protection, and the wild livestock was destroyed. Sugar plantation interests and government agencies began the reforestation of previously wasted areas with native and imported species of trees. Norfolk Island pine, ironwood, eucalyptus, and even redwood are some of the introduced tree species used in reforestation.

Many of the trails described in this book lead through such plantings, now grown into large forests. Other trails located in the most inaccessible and unfrequented regions of the Hawaiian Islands lead higher to forests largely untouched by this devastation. Sadly, even there, extinction gains ground.

Dangers, Pests, and Precautions

The wet regions of the Hawaiian Islands are mostly covered by impenetrable vegetation, and the topograghy of many portions of the islands can be exceptionally rough. Know where you came from at all times. If a trail dwindles away, it is probably a false one, such as a dead-ending hunters' route. Retrace your steps to see if you have missed the correct trail. Above all, STAY ON THE TRAIL. The rock is universally rotten and portable handholds abound; cliffs and thick vegetation make cross-country travel unwise. Off the trail, hunters may mistake you for an animal. Vegetation may crowd in and hide drop-offs. If totally lost or stranded, it is usually safest to wait for day and attract help. If you attempt to find your own way out, it is usually better to follow ridges, since the going and visibility there may be better than in gulches. Rain, even far upstream, may make streams impassable or cause flash floods. Beware of falling rocks in waterfalls. Hikers following the sea coast should not be lulled into thinking that all waves are the same size. "Rogue" waves, far larger than usual, occasionally sweep the unwary into the sea. Tidal waves sweep the beaches at rare intervals. If you experience an earthquake near the sea, run uphill immediately.

Mosquitoes are comparative newcomers to the Hawaiian Islands. The first species were introduced in the early 1800's, reputedly by whalers who emptied contaminated water casks brought ashore for refilling. Relatively few species of mosquitoes are present, and not all ecological niches are filled; thus, few are encountered above 2,800 feet, and all species tend to avoid strong sunlight. In low areas, breezy dry spots are best for camping. The local mosquitoes are not as suicidally ferocious as those found in more northerly latitudes. In time, however, even these rapacious pests may be carelessly introduced. Mosquitoes have been the factor most limiting to the survival of native forest birds. Due to avian malaria spread by mosquitoes, most native forest birds are surviving only above the elevations where mosquitoes thrive. Black widow spiders are found in Hawaii, as in all states. Poisonous centipedes and scorpions are occasionally found near sea level and can inflict stings about as painful as bee stings. No dangerous land snakes are present. Pigs may attack, if disturbed. Sharks in the waters off the beaches are not noted for being man-eaters; however, some have broken this general rule. Waves and currents are a more real danger.

Water, food, compass, current maps, and the usual emergency and first aid gear should be carried. A flashlight is especially important on late afternoon hikes. Because of the low latitude, night descends with unexpected rapidity. Allow ample time to arrive before nightfall.

Even flowing water may be contaminated by upstream animals and human beings. It is safest to treat it. Poison oak and poison ivy are not found on the Hawaiian Islands; however, some persons are allergic to the mango tree and its fruit. The bark of the paper bark tree is highly irritating when wet and should not be used for toilet paper. Numerous plants can be poisonous, if eaten, used for cooking skewers, or rubbed into skin.

Crime and violence have increased in Hawaii, just as in the rest of the United States. Hikers and especially campers are not immune. Theft is a major problem, particularly in areas frequented by tourists. Valuables should not be left unattended or left locked in cars. Vehicles left unattended are sometimes broken into or damaged. Marijuana patches must be strictly avoided since they may be jealously and dangerously guarded. The patches are usually carefully hidden and are less likely to be found along well-traveled trails. This is yet another reason to stay on the known trails.

Hiking on the more hazardous trails and camping should be in groups of three or more. Leave your plans with a responsible person. Respect private property and stay out of *kapu* (closed) watersheds or military areas. Pack out whatever you bring in. Clean your shoes and clothes to avoid spreading seeds.

Fires

In the warm lowland climate campfires add little comfort. Firewood is scarce at higher, cooler elevations and fires outside of designated firepits are wisely prohibited in the national parks and most other areas. If cooking cannot be dispensed with, a gas stove should be used. Purchase stove fuel locally, since airlines forbid its presence on planes. Fire danger is great and caution with fires cannot be stressed enough. Rain forest conditions give a false sense of security. Sunny skies and steady winds can dry up a rain-soaked morning forest and, through someone's carelessness, turn it into a blazing inferno by midafternoon. Heavy underbrush, steep slopes, high winds, and peat soils make fires extremely difficult to control. Dry humus and accumulated material on the ground is often so deep that a fire can start, burn through a wet top layer, and progress underground to burst out later and devastate large areas.

Transportation

Reduced fares may be available for interisland jet flights in connection with flights from the mainland, if booked simultaneously. It is unnecessary to reverse tracks to see the island chain, since there are direct flights between the mainland and several islands. Reduced fares may also be available for off-hour flights, standbys, and military personnel. The small planes used by some airlines fly at low elevations, thus allowing good visibility. Flights by the north coast of Molokai and the north coast of Hawaii are particularly scenic.

Bus transportation is extensive on Oahu, limited on Hawaii, and, at present, very limited or unavailable elsewhere. Hitchhiking, though possibly illegal, is fairly common. Rental cars are available on all the islands with rates varying widely. Rental agencies occasionally refuse to rent to campers and hikers.

Use of the Book

At the beginning of each island section is a road map on which the approximate locations of the trailheads are marked by trail numbers within diamonds. The trails are described in the text and illustrated by overlaid reproductions of U.S. Geological Survey topographical maps. The main trail is marked by a solid black line, the starts of side trails by a single line of dots or dashes, and roadways by double dashed lines. All the maps have true north at the top. Magnetic north lies about 11½° northeast of true north. Most maps have 40-foot contour intervals, a few have 80-foot intervals. On the upper left-hand corner of each trail description there is statistical information on the trail, a list of maps covering the area, and the name of the jurisdiction within which the trail lies. Copies of complete maps may be obtained by writing the U.S. Geological Survey, Denver Federal Center, Bldg. 41, Denver, CO 80225. Mileage has been marked along each trail and the total for the hike is included in the statistical summary. The hours given for the hikes are based on estimated hiking time for an average hiker.

The calories given for each hike represent the total number that an average 150-pound hiker would burn up for the complete hike. The number is computed by a complex formula including time, distance, grade, and trail condition as variables. It is most useful as a device for comparing the physical difficulty of the trails. Some hikers, of course, may wish to consider the number of calories to determine the degree to which they may later, in good conscience, indulge in rich foods. For example, the Akaka Falls Trail might justify only a bit of extra sweetening in one's coffee, whereas a trip up Mauna Loa via Red Hill would go far to adjust the excesses of an entire holiday season.

A subjective indication of the difficulty of the trails from an overall standpoint has been indicated by grading the trails "A," "B," and "C." Most persons can easily follow "A" trails to the end. "B" trails are a bit harder physically, and may involve more significant obstacles or hazards. "C" trails are the most physically taxing and hazardous and should be attempted only by the most experienced hikers in the best physical condition.

The highest elevation reached on the trail is shown to give an idea of the temperatures and the amount of rain that might be encountered. The elevation gain or loss on the outward leg of the trail is also described.

The distances, times, routes, and other facts in this book should be considered as estimates only. Descriptions of the trails and other information can at times be subjective and subject to confusion, and, most important, all conditions can change. This book, though hopefully a useful and generally an accurate aid, must not be relied upon to be always accurate or complete. Hikers are expected to rely on their own experience, preparation, and good on-the-spot judgement for their safety. Consult those in whose jurisdiction a trail lies for current and additional information. Addresses are at the end of this introduction.

Permits, Camping, and Current Information

Trailhead registration is sometimes required for hiking. Modest fees and advance permission or reservations are usually required to use camping areas and cabins. Plan early with the offices of the administering agencies listed in the statistical data in the trail descriptions.

Campgrounds are found throughout the state and are administered by the National Park Service, the State of Hawaii, counties, and private organizations. Camping areas close to the trails have been mentioned, but there are many more. Some campgrounds have a poor reputation for public safety. Conditions change rapidly, so discuss plans with and obtain additional printed information from the appropriate agency.

Island of Hawaii

Hawaii Volcanoes National Park
Hawaii, HI 96718
(808) 967-7311

Pu'uhonua-o-Honaunau National
Historical Park
Honaunau, Kona, HI 96726
(808) 328-2288

Division of Forestry and Wildlife
P.O. Box 4849
Hilo, HI 96720
(808) 961-7221

Division of State Parks
P.O. Box 936
Hilo, HI 96721
(808) 961-7200

Department of Parks and Recreation
County of Hawaii
25 Aupuni Street
Hilo, HI 96720
(808) 961-8311

Island of Maui

Haleakala National Park
P.O. Box 537
Makawao, Maui, HI 96768
(808) 572-9306

Division of Forestry and Wildlife
P.O. Box 1015
Wailuku, Maui, HI 96793
(808) 244-4352

Division of State Parks
P.O. Box 1049
Wailuku, Maui, HI 96793
(808) 244-4352

Department of Parks and Recreation
County of Maui
1580 Kaahumanu Avenue
Wailuku, Maui, HI 96793
(808) 244-5514

Island of Lanai

Koele Company
P.O. Box L
Island of Lanai, HI 96763
(808) 565-6661

Island of Molokai

Division of Forestry and Wildlife
P.O. Box 347
Kaunakai, Molokai, HI 96748
(808) 244-4352

Division of State Parks
P.O. Box 153
Kaunakakai, Molokai, HI 96748
(808) 567-6083

County Beach Parks
Department of Public Works
Kaunakakai, Molokai, HI 96748
(808) 553-3221

Island of Oahu

Division of Forestry and Wildlife
1151 Punchbowl Street
Honolulu, HI 96813
(808) 548-8850

Division of State Parks
P.O. Box 621
Honolulu, HI 96809
(808) 548-7455

Department of Parks and Recreation
City and County of Honolulu
650 South King Street
Honolulu, HI 96813
(808) 523-4525

Island of Kauai

Division of Forestry and Wildlife
P.O. Box 1671
Lihue, Kauai, HI 96766
(808) 245-4433

Division of State Parks
P.O. Box 1671
Lihue, Kauai, HI 96766
(808) 245-4444

Department of Parks and Recreation
County of Kauai
4444 Rice Street
Lihue, Kauai 96766
(808) 245-8821

Kokee Lodge, Manager
P.O. Box 819
Waimea, Kauai, HI 96796
(808) 335-6061

Island of Hawaii

Ancient Hawaiian legend relates that Pele, the Polynesian goddess of volcanoes, made her early home in Kauai. Dissatisfied, she moved south along the chain of islands, eventually residing in the southeastern portion of the Island of Hawaii. Interestingly, this path follows geologic history. The Hawaiian island chain was formed by volcanism from northwest to southeast. Some geologists argue that the volcanoes erupted along a fault line. Others contend that one island after another was formed as the earth's crust gradually moved northwest over a stationary hot spot far beneath the earth's surface. In any event, this volcanism created the Island of Hawaii and in the process provided unmatched hiking experiences.

The 4,038-square-mile Island of Hawaii has 63 percent of all the land area of the Hawaiian Islands. The trails are generally longer than those on the other islands, and the scale of the land forms is far larger. However, since Hawaii is the newest of the islands, it has not yet experienced the full effects of erosion. Large, lava-covered areas, especially in the west, are quite barren. They may be dry because of the rain shadows of the island's volcanic mountains or because the mountains are too far above the rain clouds borne by the trade winds. Furthermore, the lava is still so new that deep soil has not had a chance to form and water quickly disappears below the surface. The unique native forests that once did retain water and covered many areas have been largely destroyed by grazing animals.

The Island of Hawaii was formed by five great volcanoes: Mauna Loa, Mauna Kea, Hualalei, Kilauea, and Kohala. Of these

Fresh lava — first plants

only the oldest, Kohala, has eroded as much as the volcanoes on the older islands such as Kauai and Oahu. The most spectacular valleys and waterfalls are in the Kohala Mountains. The lower north and east slopes of Mauna Kea are somewhat less eroded, but still offer pleasant waterfalls and pools. The Akaka Falls Trail leads to one of the most scenic of these waterfalls.

Active examples of the geologic processes that formed all of the Hawaiian Islands are found in Hawaii Volcanoes National Park. Park trails lead past volcanic vents, over still-cooling lava, and to the top of world's largest shield volcano. The Kilauea Iki Trail leads into one of the most volcanically active parts of the world. It is so active that

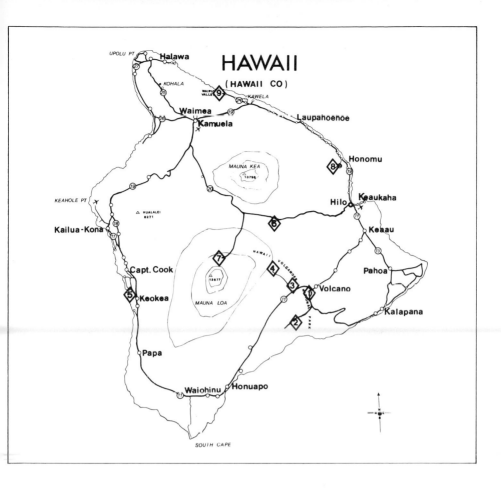

HAWAII
(HAWAII CO)

volcanism will perhaps soon destroy the trail itself. The trails up Mauna Loa are more like mountain climbs than hikes, since they lead into high, frigid regions devoid of plant and animal life. Careful preparation is required because the cold can be extreme and because of the danger of serious sunburn. The great elevation and distances of these trails make them exhausting, but also unforgettable.

Two trails, Puu Oo and Kipuka Puaulu (Bird Park), lead through another type of volcanic phenomenon, the *kipuka,* which is an area undamaged by surrounding flows of lava. Protected by the rough surrounding lava from some of the worst depredations of livestock, kipukas provide good opportunities to observe rare native Hawaiian plants and birds.

The Halape Trail in Hawaii Volcanoes National Park leads steeply down extensive

Headlands west of Waimanu Valley

29

Halape after the earthquake

lava flows to Halape's crescent-shaped white-sand beach, formed after the earthquake and tidal wave of 1975. Among the breakers lies the site of the idyllic grove of coconut trees that once graced Halape.

Camping is excellent and safest in Hawaii Volcanoes National Park. The park headquarters provides current information on the well-cared-for campgrounds, cabins, and wilderness campsites.

The Waipio-Waimanu Trail leads along the base of the rugged Kohala Mountains into an area as isolated as any in the Hawaiian Islands. There, large valleys which once teemed with people and were centers of civilization are now almost empty. The trail passes by the ruins of ancient Hawaiian villages and through abandoned groves of fruit trees. It ends at long, beautiful, black-sand Waimanu Beach.

Kipuka forest — Puu Oo Trail

Thurston Lava Tube

1. Kilauea Iki

2½-hour loop
500 calories; difficulty B
3-mile loop
Highest point: 3900 feet
Elevation loss: 400 feet
Maps: Kilauea Crater, Volcano 1:24,000
Hawaii Volcanoes National Park

Kilauea Iki means "little Kilauea." It is almost a scale model of large Kilauea Crater, located just to the west. Although smaller, it has provided spectacular volcanic shows. The Kilauea Iki Trail has been selected from several interesting trails across the floors and along the rims of both craters because it offers in a short distance varied and impressive evidence of Hawaii's volcanism.

Kilauea Iki is world famous for the great eruption of 1959 in which a lava fountain at one point reached 1900 feet high. Spewing from the southwest side of Kilauea Iki, it half filled the crater and put on a spectacular display for 36 days. Films of this eruption are shown hourly at park headquarters.

Route: Drive 29 miles southwest of Hilo on Highway 11 to Hawaii Volcanoes National Park. Turn off left to the park headquarters one mile after passing the park entrance. From the park headquarters proceed on Crater Rim Road south (left) approximately 1.5 miles to the Kilauea Iki overlook on the west (right) side of the road. Parking is available at the overlook, and the trailhead is clearly marked on the north end of the parking lot. Walk counterclockwise along the north rim of Kilauea Iki Crater, passing junctions with other trails in the area. About 0.7 miles from the trailhead, the trail descends through a handsome forest of tree ferns. One mile from the trailhead, it joins a connector to the Byron Ledge Trail. A short side trip on the Byron Ledge Trail offers an impressive view of Kilauea Crater. From the junction with the Byron Ledge Trail, the Kilauea Iki Trail starts side-hilling down the wall of Kilauea Iki Crater onto its floor and past the vent of the 1959 lava fountain. Many ohelo bushes, loaded with succulent red berries in the summer, may be found along the way. These berries are one of the earliest plants to appear after volcanic activity has scorched the ground. Tradition has it that you must offer some of the berries to Pele, the goddess of volcanism, before eating any or you will incur her wrath. Since at this point you are about to walk across almost a mile of still-cooling lava, past a dormant volcanic vent, you might consider this tradition carefully.

Past the vent, the trail leads across the crater's flat floor on lava which sends up clouds of steam where water reaches the still-hot rocks beneath the surface. Note how ferns and small mosses are slowly pioneering this area. Proceed directly across the crater to its east side where a stone cairn marks the trail up the east wall. The trail switchbacks through a forest of giant tree ferns and ends at Crater Rim Road and a junction with the Crater Rim Trail. Immediately across the road a 0.3-mile loop trail leads to and through Thurston Lava Tube, a worthwhile side trip. Return to your starting point by following the Crater Rim Trail along the rim of Kilauea Iki for 0.3 miles.

Kilauea Iki Crater

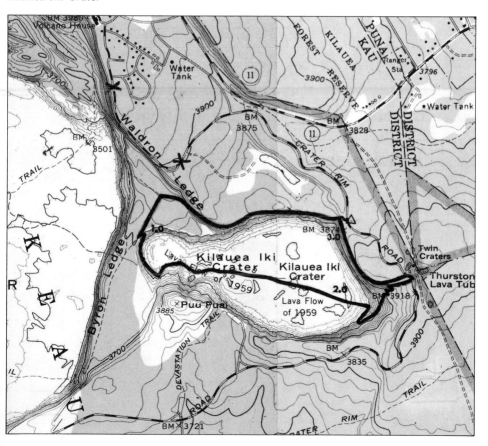

2. Halape

2 days; 4 hours down, 6 hours up
3000 calories; difficulty C
7.2 miles one way
Highest point: 2920 feet
Elevation loss: 2920 feet
Maps: Kau Desert,
      Makaopuhi Crater 1:24,000
Hawaii Volcanoes National Park

Located in Hawaii Volcanoes National Park on the hot, dry, south shore of the "Big Island" and reached by a long, dry trail, Halape and its extensive stand of coconut palms was reminiscent of some Arabian oasis. But now, idyllic, old Halape, where many a leisurely day was spent beneath its palms, is no more. The great earthquake of November, 1975, caused the land to drop beneath the sea. Within seconds, in the dark hours of early morning, a huge tidal wave rolled inland, overtaking startled campers and overflowing the land. Afterwards the battered dead trunks of Halape's once lovely grove stood among the breakers. A crescent-shaped white-sand beach and a green lagoon formed. Young coconut trees give promise of a new Halape, perhaps lovelier than the first.

Old Halape

Route: Having registered for wilderness camping at the Hawaii Volcanoes National Park headquarters (see directions on page 26) take Crater Rim Road or its replacement south about three miles around Kilauea Iki Crater to Chain of Craters Road. Follow Chain of Craters Road south for 2.5 miles to its junction with Hilina Pali Road. From this junction follow Hilina Pali Road five miles to Kipuka Nene picnic area. This area has water tanks, restrooms, and a picnic pavilion. The trail starts at the back of the pavilion and heads south on a dirt road now closed to vehicles. After following the dirt road for over two miles the trail turns south down toward the ocean, leaving the main dirt road for good and soon changing from dirt road to trail. About 5.5 miles from the shelter, the Hilina Pali Trail enters from the west near Puu Kapukapu, a hillock to the southwest. Proceed past this

Halape after the earthquake

junction down to Halape and its new shelter about 200 yards from the sea.

Brackish, unsafe water is located at Halape in a large crack 75 yards directly inland from the beach. Water may be available from a tank at the shelter. Impressive evidence of the great geologic forces that changed the area will be visible for many years. The shadeless hike uphill to Kipuka Nene can be hot. It is best to return in the early morning or late afternoon and carry ample supplies of water. Afternoon hikers should take flashlights since they may be overtaken by darkness.

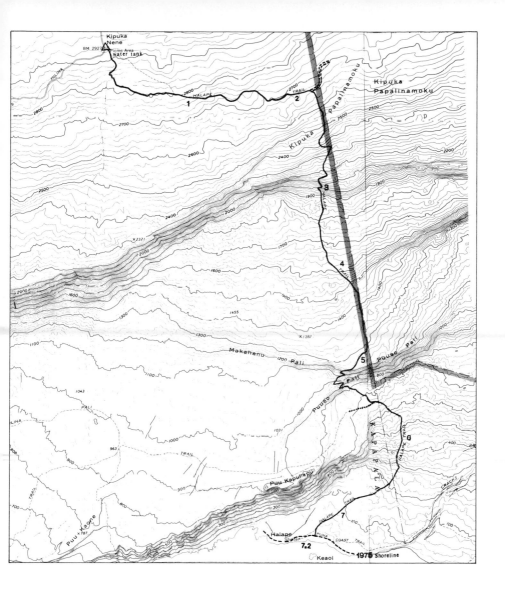

Pioneering grass along Halape Trail

3. Kipuka Puaulu (Bird Park)

1-hour loop
200 calories; difficulty A
1.2-mile loop
Highest point: 4175 feet
Elevation gain: 250 feet
Map: Kilauea Crater 1:24,000
Hawaii Volcanoes National Park

This trail provides an easy opportunity to view a *kipuka* (an area missed by surrounding lava flows) and a largely unspoiled native Hawaiian forest. This kipuka, like kipukas at higher, less verdant elevations along the Puu Oo Trail (described later), provides numerous examples of native Hawaiian plants and related animals. The National Park Service has done a commendable job of maintaining the trail and labeling the plants for visitors. A booklet written by the Hawaii Natural History Association describing the labeled plants on this self-guided trail is available at the park headquarters.

Route: To reach the trailhead from Hilo, drive 31 miles southwest on Highway 11 to Mauna Loa Road, located about 2.3 miles past the Hawaii Volcanoes National Park headquarters turnoff. Follow Mauna Loa Road 1.6 miles to the parking area next to the trailhead. The trailhead is well marked with a display of some of the more common plants and birds you will see during this pleasant, easy hike. The grade is gradual, the route is obvious and the path is well maintained.

Near the display, the trail passes through a fence designed to keep out wild pigs. Close this gate since it is protection for this fragile area from these animals. Just beyond the gate the path joins the loop. Take the left-hand fork around the loop's gentle course. After 0.5 miles, a short side trail leads left (north) to a large koa tree, about 50 yards off the trail. From this turn-off the rest of the loop returns generally downhill to the starting point. Numerous native Hawaiian birds may be seen in the nearby treetops during the hike. The most common

Giant ohia tree

is the apapane, a little, bright-red bird with black wings and tail. It is especially fond of the nectar of the red-blossomed ohia lehua trees. The iiwi bird, also fairly common, is colored like the apapane, but is somewhat larger and has a curved bill. These birds and others are best seen early in the morning or at evening, especially after a rain.

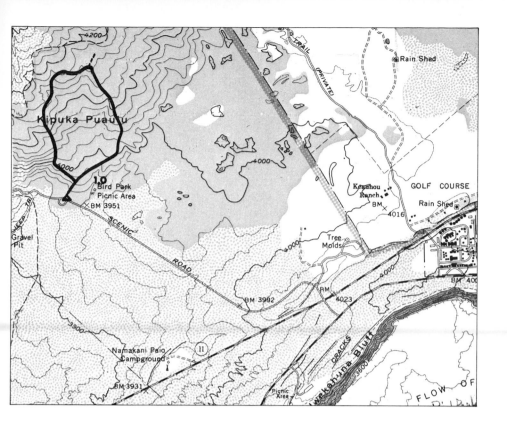

Kipuka Puaulu Trail

4. Mauna Loa Trail (via Red Hill)

2 days up, 1-2 days down
18 hours up, 12 hours down
8700 calories; difficulty C
18.3 miles one way
Highest point: 13,250 feet
Elevation gain: 6,600 feet
Maps: Kipuka Pakekake, Kookoolau,
      Mauna Loa, Puu Ulaulu 1:24,000
Hawaii Volcanoes National Park

In terms of physical effort, the climb up the Mauna Loa Trail via Red Hill to Mauna Loa Cabin is one of the hardest hikes in the Hawaiian Islands. It is also perhaps the most memorable. Mauna Loa's volume is enormous — on the order of 10,000 cubic miles. Mt. Shasta, by comparison, has a volume of only 80 cubic miles. Mauna Loa (long mountain) and Mauna Kea (white mountain) are the highest mountains in the world — if one takes the elevation starting from their bases on the ocean floor. From the ocean floor, the mountains rise approximately 30,000 feet to their summits, making each formation taller than Mt. Everest. Even with a head start at 6,662 feet above sea level, it is truly a long, long way to the top of Mauna Loa.

It is said of Mount Fuji, "He who does not climb Fuji once is a fool; he who climbs it twice is also a fool." Some would say the same of Mauna Loa. The written word, however, cannot express the experience of hiking along the great northeast rift of Mauna Loa, past mile upon mile of iridescent ash. Nor can words express the experience of rising before dawn and watching the faintly increasing morning light creep across huge Mokuaweoweo Caldera, a great lake of still steaming lava which melts every few years to run down the mountain and build further the Island of Hawaii. Not a living thing is in view. The air is cold and rare.

Route: Drive southwest on Highway 11 from Hilo to the Hawaii Volcanoes National Park headquarters. You must register with the rangers there for the climb and for use of both Red Hill Cabin, halfway along the trail, and Mauna Loa Cabin, located on

South across Mokuaweoweo Caldera

the east side of Mokuaweoweo Caldera. These cabins are equipped with mattresses and bunks. You need halazone tablets for purifying the water which may have been collected from the cabin roofs. Check with the rangers for current information and regarding the suitability of your equipment, including heavy wool clothing and sleeping bag (in plastic sacks), rain gear, goggles for snow, water, food, flashlight, sunburn protection, and other mountaineering equipment.

Arctic conditions with considerable snow, extreme cold, fog, and high winds and rain can occur at any time of year on Mauna Loa. The weather may be cloudy for days at a time and the trail obscured by snow. Molten lava and noxious fumes may spew out unexpectedly from volcanic vents underlying the mountain. The rough *aa* lava off the trail is torturesome going. Take into account the effect of elevation along the upper portions of this trail. Nearly everyone living close to sea level is affected by exertion at these altitudes near 13,000 feet. Consider the miles at these altitudes to be twice as long as those at sea level. Headaches, pounding heart, and rapid breathing are indications of the effects of altitude; the only immediate remedy is rest and more oxygen. The rough lava along this trail will quickly destroy all but heavy boots.

From the park headquarters, drive on Highway 11 west, about 2.3 miles to the start of Mauna Loa Road and follow it to the end. Mauna Loa Road climbs for 11 miles to end near the 6,662 foot level at a waterless lookout and parking area. The trailhead is located just uphill from the lookout. The trail at first contours east across the slope for a short distance, then passes uphill through a gate. Close this gate to prevent damage to the park by wild goats. After the gate the trail leads up through steadily diminishing vegetation to Red Hill Cabin 7.0 miles (4-6 hours) from the trailhead. For its entire extent the trail is easy to follow unless covered by snow or obscured by poor visibility. It is marked by the passage of others and *ahu* (stone cairns) located at intervals.

From Red Hill Cabin, which is the first night's resting place, the trail leads up through land almost devoid of vegetation and covered with lava flows of bizarre shapes and colors, past splatter cones and across large volcanic faults to Mauna Loa Cabin approximately 11.3 miles (12 hours) away. The trail from Red Hill is in the path of the 1984 flows. Follow the most recent ahu markers to find the most accurate route. There is no water readily available along this trail and the lower portions can

Mauna Loa Trail going over pahoehoe lava

be hot and dry. At 16.3 miles from the start, the trail reaches North Pit, the northern "bay" of the great Mokuaweoweo Caldera. There, four trails intersect. The Summit Trail leads to the right along the caldera's west rim to the summit. The Observatory Trail leads to the right (north), down to the Observatory. The Cabin Trail (considered here as part of the Mauna Loa Trail) leads south across North Pit to Mauna Loa Cabin on the east side of the caldera.

In former years this cabin was reached by another trail, now abandoned, which followed the caldera's east rim. The older trail is now poorly marked and is by no means as interesting as the route across the floor of North Pit. The trail to the cabin across North Pit drops a short distance to the pit floor and then leads straight south across the smooth, flat lava. After crossing the pit floor, the trail leads up and generally south to Mokuaweoweo Caldera's rim, skirting the southwest rim of Lua Poholo, a deep secondary caldera. The trail then continues along the caldera's rim to the cabin. About 0.3 miles due south of the cabin, ice and snow may often be found in a crevice marked by ahu.

If caught by darkness on a clear summer night, follow the trail across the caldera by setting a course on the Southern Cross, visible close to the horizon. Do not stumble into Lua Poholo in the dark. Approach its rim and all other such formations with caution.

Stay the second night at the cabin. From it you may wish to take the climb to Mauna Loa's summit, retracing your steps to the junction of the Mauna Loa Summit Trail with the trail to the cabin. From the junction follow the signed trail, marked with ahu, along the west rim of the caldera to the summit. The nine-mile round trip at these altitudes should be considered an all-day affair, though route-finding is no problem. As an alternative, explore the southwest portion of the caldera near South Pit, which has lava flows and fields of golden pumice from volcanism in the 1940's.

Be sure to inform the park headquarters of your return. Failure to do so is unforgivable.

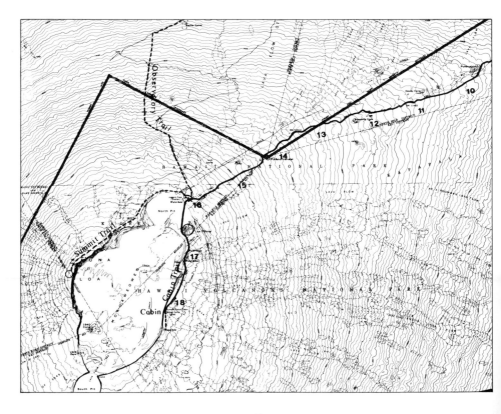

Red Hill Cabin

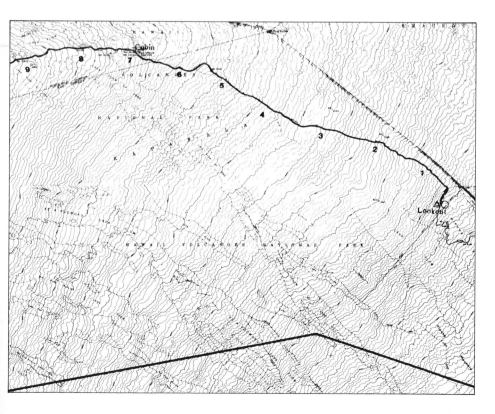

5. Pu'uhonua-o-Honaunau

2-hour loop
300 calories; difficulty A
1.6-mile loop
Highest point: 40 feet
Elevation gain: 40 feet
Map: Honaunau 1:24,000
Pu'uhonua-o-Honaunau National Historical Park

Ramp over Keanae'e Cliff

Pu'uhonua-o-Honaunau National Park preserves the ancient ruins of several heiau, fish ponds, house foundations, sled ramps, trails from different periods of Hawaiian history, and a great stone wall, within whose boundaries *kapu* breakers and the vanquished could find refuge. From the visitor center a short interpretive trail meanders by re-created models of ancient houses, fearsome wooden carvings, and the impressive stonework.

Beyond the interpretive area, lie the routes of an early foot path and a nine-teenth century horse trail leading south to a stone ramp over Keanae'e Cliff. In the early days Keanae'e Cliff, with its "frozen water-fall" of lava, was an obstacle to travelers along this coast. It was passable only at a low point where the cliff meets Alahaka Bay. The prehistoric foot trail of the type marked by a single row of smooth stones reached the cliff at this low point after hugging the coast to avoid dreaded *kapu* areas. With the introduction of horses and the end of the *kapu* system, a new, more direct, inland horse trail, was built, marked by "kerbstones" on either side. South of Keanae'e's housesites the new trail basically followed the ancient foot trail. This was probably the route mentioned in Mark Twain's letters about the area. The substantial ramp now climbing the cliff was built around 1868. For more information about the old trails, see *Trails* by Russell A. Apple, Bishop Museum Press.

Route: This seaside park is located on the Kona (leeward, west) coast at the bottom of the road descending 1000 feet in three miles from the turnoff at the Keokea intersection on Highway 11. The loop through the inter-pretive area begins at the visitor center and is described in materials provided by the park.

To reach the points of interest farther south, proceed along the road from the visitor center to the seaside picnic area and then about a third of a mile south along the shore until shortly before the shoreline is indented by Alahaka Bay. There, about 100 paces inland, past various stonework, is the straight, level 1871 horse trail. Proceed south from this junction to climb the ramp. The trail then eventually passes out of the park area. A narrow, perhaps dangerous, lava tube starts immediately on the left side of the ramp and leads under it to the sea.

The 1871 trail leading straight north from the ramp provides a good return route, passing by prospering introduced dryland plants which, being unpalatable, stickery, or poisonous, have defied the appetites of goats and cattle. It soon crosses the course of a rock sled ramp seen lying uphill on the right. When covered with pili grass and mud in ancient times the ramp must have been the scene of many a merry slide. In an act eloquently bespeaking the new age, the royal sled ramp was partially demolished to provide fill rock for the horse trail.

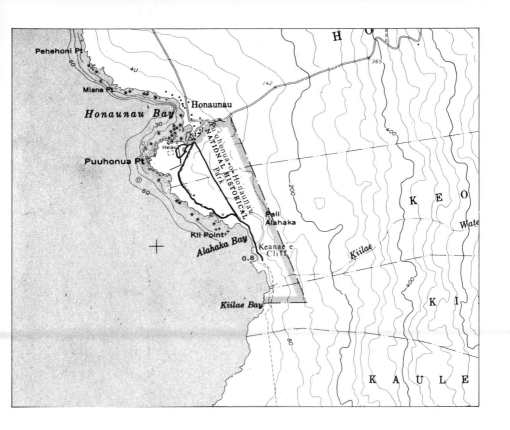

Kapu

6. Puu Oo Trail

2 hours in, 2 hours out
1100 calories; difficulty B
3.7 miles one way
Highest point: 5800 feet
Elevation gain: 200 feet
Maps: Kulani, Upper Piihonua,
         Puu Oo 1:24,000
Division of Forestry and Wildlife

Hawaii is a young volcanic island, growing at a high rate by the standards of geologic time. Lava flows have frequently covered large areas of the island even in recent years. One such area, located in the Ainahou and Upper Waiakea Forest Reserves, is traversed by the Puu Oo Trail, which provides excellent examples of the return of vegetation to areas covered by lava flows.

The most recent volcanic activity seems to be limited to areas farther south, in Hawaii Volcanoes National Park, but the flows crossed by the Puu Oo Trail are by no means ancient.

Early cattle ranchers had to use the trail to drive their herds over the rough, scoriaceous lava beds of *aa* (rough) lava that separated the saddle lands between Mauna Kea and Mauna Loa, where their cattle grazed, from the market at the seaport of Hilo. Although Hilo is not far from this region, as the crow flies, the only practical way through the *aa* lava led down the Puu Oo Trail to the town of Volcano near Hawaii Volcanoes National Park. From there the cattle could be driven on down the road to Hilo or, in still earlier times, to the ocean to the south. The trail has not been used for this purpose for many years. Yet, it may still be followed by looking closely for the *ahu* (stone cairns) and other trail markers.

The trail crosses the lava flows of 1855, 1881, and 1935, among others, which provide good examples of both *aa* and *pahoehoe* (smooth) lava. Different types and thicknesses of vegetation grow on each of these flows depending on the age of the flow and the type of lava. The trail also

Pahoehoe lava

crosses large *kipukas* where the lava flows have by-passed the old growth of ohia, pukeawe, ohelo, and majestic koa trees, populated with a wide assortment of endemic bird species. Native ferns, lichens, and mosses are found along the way. Rainfall in the area is up to 80 inches a year, but the land appears quite dry because of the good drainage of the underlying lava. Since few people take this trail, and ohelo berries are abundant, bird watching is well rewarded, especially early in the morning and toward evening. Native birds, such as the apapane, iiwi, and amakihi abound. There is even a chance of seeing the rare nene goose.

Route: Take Saddle Road (Highway 200) west from Hilo until about 0.4 miles after the 22 mile marker, near the boundary of the Ainahou and the Upper Waiakea Forest Reserves. The trail begins on the left (south) side of the highway. A wooden sign marks the trailhead. Parking is available.

Follow the trail from the parking area south along a course roughly parallel to and west of a powerline and service road which

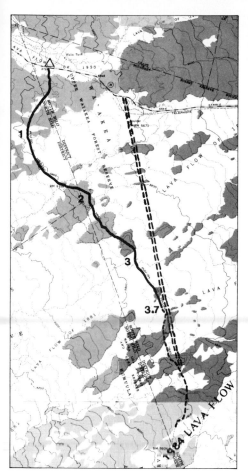

Amaumau fern (sadleria)

are visible in the distance. The trail is difficult to follow at points. Look for *ahu* and other signs of the trail, being quick to retrace your steps if lost. After about 3.7 miles the trail joins the powerline road. This is a good turnaround point since you have already passed the most interesting portion of the trail. Further on, the trail has been obliterated by the 1984 lava flows and permission may be required for access. From the turnaround point you have the option of returning via the powerline road and the Saddle Road. Since the trail is located at nearly 6000 feet, it can be cool and you should dress warmly. There is neither potable water nor a campground on the trail.

7. Observatory Trail

2 days; 8-12 hours up, 6 hours down
3500 calories; difficulty C
6 miles one way
Highest point: 13,250 feet
Elevation gain: 2,250 feet
Maps: Kokoolau, Mauna Loa, 1:24,000
Hawaii Volcanoes National Park

A road from the north leading to the 11,000-foot level provides access to the lesser used of the two routes for climbing to Mauna Loa Cabin on the east rim of the Mokuaweoweo Caldera. The trail does not follow a rift zone and, therefore, is not as interesting geologically as the Mauna Loa Trail (via Red Hill), which is the recommended route. It does, however, offer good views of Mauna Kea. The climb is long. It is best to start walking at first light and in any event not later than early morning.

Route: Register for the climb and the cabin with the Hawaii Volcanoes National Park headquarters. Check the suitability of your equipment with the rangers, obtain from them the latest information on access and conditions, read this book's description of the Mauna Loa Trail (via Red Hill), and check park literature for more information regarding equipment and hazards.

Drive on Highway 200 (Saddle Road) to the west, about 27 miles from Hilo. Turn off to the south onto a paved road just before reaching Puu Huluhulu, a small but prominent wooded cone to the left of the highway and shortly before the turnoff to Humuula Sheep Station. This road leads for 17 miles through barren lava fields to a weather observatory located at 11,000 feet on the side of Mauna Loa. The road forks about 8 miles from its start. Keep to the paved, right fork. Drive until the observatory comes into view, but park about 300 yards below it where a rough, four-wheel-drive road leads off to the right. No water is available at the trailhead or along the trail.

Follow this road on foot for about 800 yards to the signed trailhead and then follow the *ahu* (rock cairns) and orange-

Morning climb

yellow markers, which lead directly up the mountainside on flows of *pahoehoe* (smooth) lava. You will also encounter *aa* (rough) lava on this trail. After about two miles the trail veers somewhat easterly (left) and joins the four-wheel-drive road, passing a locked gate before it leaves to continue more directly up, over ash and *pahoehoe* lava flows. It then recrosses the road and after a considerable climb reaches a junction of trails on the northeast side of North Pit. Periodic lava flows may cover this area and alter the course of the trails. The Summit Trail leads west (right) up to the summit. The Mauna Loa Trail leads northeast, down to Mauna Loa Road via Red Hill. The Cabin Trail (considered here as an extension of the Observatory Trail) leads south across North Pit to Mauna Loa Cabin on the east side of the caldera. Take the Cabin Trail down a short incline to the floor of North Pit. The trail follows *ahu* straight south across the smooth floor of North Pit. It then climbs generally south to the caldera rim, skirting the southwest rim of Lua Poholo, a deep secondary crater. If overtaken by darkness on a clear summer

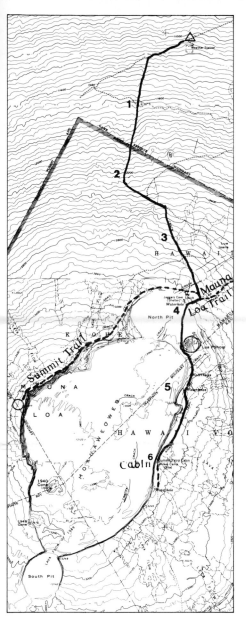

View north to Mauna Kea

sickness more likely on this route. Wear stout boots, preferably expendable ones, for this rough lava. Heavy wool clothing, windbreakers, waterproofs, goggles for snow, sunburn protection, and other mountaineering equipment must be taken. Landmarks are few before reaching the caldera; thus, traveling in uncertain weather or in winter can be perilous and should be avoided.

night, set your course generally on the Southern Cross. Be careful not to fall into Lua Poholo. After passing Lua Poholo, the trail follows along the east rim of the caldera, reaching Mauna Loa Cabin about 1.5 miles past Lua Poholo Crater.

This route is only slightly less difficult physically than the route up from Red Hill, since at these altitudes the thin air makes the miles seem twice as long as at sea level. The rapid gain in elevation makes altitude

8. Akaka Falls

1/2-hour loop
150 calories; difficulty A
0.4-mile loop
Highest point: 1200 feet
Elevation loss: 100 feet
Map: Akaka Falls 1:24,000
Division of State Parks

This leisurely half-hour hike, suitable for everyone, gives good views of Akaka and Kahuna Falls, two of the more impressive waterfalls in the Hawaiian Islands. The well-maintained trail, with steps in the steeper portions, winds gently down a ridge above the deep canyon into which Akaka and Kahuna Falls plunge. Along the way the trail weaves through dense tropical rain forest replete with epiphytes (non-parasitic plants growing on other plants) hanging from the forest canopy. Brilliant red ginger, fragrant plumeria, banana plants, hapu ferns, ti plants, and the colorful flowers of the bird of paradise make this an especially pleasant hike for a botanist or nature lover. Along the way the Division of State Parks has placed benches as resting places for hikers. You may listen to the muffled roar of the waterfalls in the distance and the occasional sounds of the birds which inhabit this lovely forest.

Route: Take Highway 19 north from Hilo and drive about 11 miles to the exit to Akaka Falls State Park on Highway 220. From that junction drive 3.7 miles to the end of the road at the state park, where ample parking is available. Overnight camping is not allowed. You may take the loop trail either clockwise or counterclockwise. If you take it counterclockwise, you will first encounter Kahuna Falls (a *kahuna* was a priest in ancient Hawaii). This beautiful falls cascades from a side canyon across the way into the main canyon below, making several drops into crystal-clear pools. You will next encounter the vista overlooking Akaka Falls (*akaka* means clear or luminous). Kahuna and Akaka Falls resulted from the variations in

Akaka Falls

strength of the underlying layers of rock. The soft, lower layers of rock erode more rapidly than the hard upper layers. As the upper layers are undercut they fall into the pool below, are broken up, and carried away by the plunging waters. In this way, Akaka Falls and others like it have moved upstream over the years.

The trail returns to the parking area through huge philodendrons which stand guard with their 2-foot leaves, making the hiker feel like an insect in the greenery. The top of the trail has well-maintained restrooms, a drinking fountain, and picnic tables with orchids hanging overhead. Even if the weather is poor, this trail is worth taking since the occasional breaks in the mist around the falls only add to the air of beauty and mystery of the location. The dense and wonderfully varying vegetation

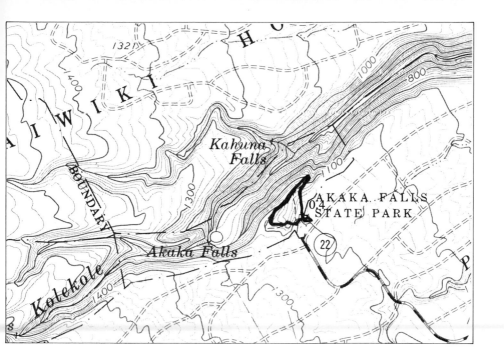

Kahuna Falls

along the trail is in itself a sufficient reason
for a visit. In addition the fragrant scents of
the rain forest and flowers growing along
the trail are much stronger on rainy days.

9. Waipio and Waimanu Valleys

2-3 days; 9 hours in, 10½ hours out
5800 calories; difficulty C
9 miles one way
Highest point: 1350 feet
Elevation loss: 3000 feet
Elevation gain: 2100 feet
Map: Honokane, Kukuihaele 1:24,000
Division of Forestry and Wildlife

The Waipio and Waimanu Valleys were centers of Hawaiian civilization in ancient times. Their verdant, well-watered floors supported rich crops of taro which fed a large population. A fertile imagination can conjure up sights of the armies of Kamehameha the Great that once marched in Waipio, the naval battle between the forces of Hawaii and Maui off the Waimanu Valley, and the meetings of the most powerful *kahuna* (ancient Hawaiian priests) in the islands. Some say that human sacrifices were made at a now-vanished *heiau* (a Hawaiian temple) near the mouth of the Waipio Valley. It is even said, somewhat ironically for so beautiful a place, that a tunnel to Hell (now covered with sand) begins somewhere in the valley. Today, but for a few taro farmers in Waipio, the valleys are unpopulated.

Route: Drive from Hilo north along Highway 19 for about 42 miles. Turn right onto Highway 240 and follow it through Honokaa for 9.5 miles to the Waipio Valley Lookout, the start of this trail. All cars except four-wheel-drive vehicles must be left at this point since the road down the east slope of the Waipio Valley is very steep. Follow this road down to the valley floor and take the first road to the right all the way to the beach. Wade Wailoa Stream, if safe, close to where it enters the sea. Cross the valley along the beach until you are within 100 yards of the northwest wall. The trail leads up the valley floor past a swampy area into the forest below the northwest wall. A second, faint trail soon intersects from the right. This is the start of the switchback ascent of the northwest wall. The trail, though rough and steep, is less

Headland west of Waimanu Valley

difficult than it looks from the Waipio Valley Lookout since it is well dug into the hillside. Here and elsewhere rain makes the footing slick and hazardous and boots with new tread should be used.

The trail reaches the ridge and contours through numerous small valleys toward the Waimanu Valley. A shelter is located about two-thirds of the way along the trail.

Use care when camping and hiking since there is extreme danger of fire along the trail, especially in the dense pads of needles under the ironwood thickets. The scars of recent forest fires illustrate previous

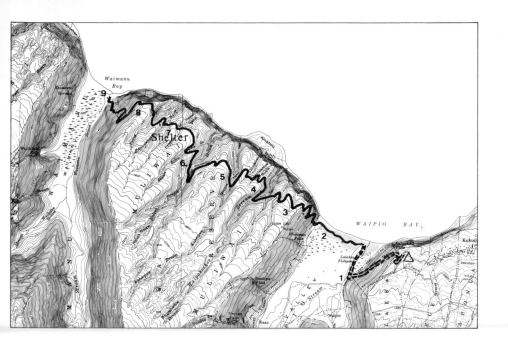

Waipio Valley

carelessness. The trail crosses thirteen low running streams to reach the rim of the Waimanu Valley. During storms these run high and travel should not be attempted.

The Waimanu Valley looks remarkably similar to the Waipio Valley, but it is somewhat smaller and without any human inhabitants. Although covered with loose rock in a few places, the trail down is generally in good shape. At the bottom of the descent, work toward the beach through groves of hala trees. Ford small Waimanu Stream on the southeast end of the beach and follow the beach to the northwest side of the valley. Water from the stream on the

valley floor may be unsafe to drink. Purer water may be obtained from the stream closest to the ocean on the northwest side of the valley; a faint trail leads to it.

A good side trip is to bushwhack up the northwest side of the valley floor through groves of mountain apple trees, laden with tasty fruit, to Waiilikahi Falls and its deep, wide pool. Wild pigs unused to human beings are numerous in this valley and care should be taken not to surprise them. If startled, they may be dangerous. Mosquitoes are plentiful and hungry. Stone walls, foundations, and terraces offer abundant evidence of the ancient civilization.

Island of Maui

Maui's colorful villages, superb scenery, and balmy weather have made it the favorite island of many visitors to the state. The pride of its residents is understandable. One must agree with even the most glowing descriptions given to the island. It is hard to imagine a lovelier place. The fame of Haleakala Crater and the Hana Coast are world-wide. Polipoli State Park, though little known, has a forest of great beauty. Best of all for hikers, these same areas contain miles of interesting trails and provide good locations for camping.

Haleakala Volcano forms the east half of the island. At its top is Haleakala Crater, actually an area formed by two great valleys which have coalesced at their heads. Volcanism later formed colorful cinder cones and lava flows on the crater floor. The crater is a central point of interest on Maui and is a national park. Three cabins are located along the well-marked and well-maintained trails that lead through the massive crater.

Two long traverses of the crater are described here, south-north by the Sliding Sands-Halemauu Trail and west-east by the Sliding Sands-Kaupo Gap Trail. These have the advantage of passing by all three cabins. They can be hiked in combination with the many side trails in the crater. Haleakala's trails, although not quite as stark as those up Mauna Loa on the Island of Hawaii, lead through regions that can be covered with snow at certain times of the year and can at any time be quite wet and cold. Vegetation is sparse; the air is thin. Water is available only at the three strategically located cabins. However, the barrenness of the region makes it all the more interesting,

papaya

because the great erosion and volcanism that shaped the crater are made apparent.

The little flowers and the fantastic silversword plant that survive in this forbidding landscape are much appreciated for their efforts. Several days can be spent exploring the crater. If you wish to use the cabins, be sure to make reservations with Haleakala National Park three months in advance. Permits to camp in the crater must be obtained at the park headquarters. A maximum of three days for any combination of cabin and campsite use in any one month is allowed. Registration boxes for

Haleakala Crater

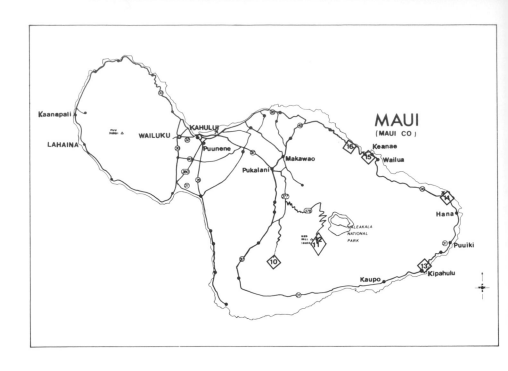

Waimoku Falls

Lava sea cliffs—
Hana-Waianapanapa Coastal Trail

Ironwood and naupaka — Hana-Waianapanapa Coastal Trail

day hikes are located at the trailheads. Obtain current information from the park regarding your plans.

Polipoli State Park, 6,000 feet high on the southwest side of Haleakala Volcano, has a complex of trails leading through an extensive forest of trees imported from more northerly latitudes. Redwood, cedar, sugi, and many other species grow here, providing scenery reminiscent of the west coast of North America. Only the most central trail is included in this book. Others are well marked and can easily be followed through this lovely region. The several campsites located among the handsome stands of redwood and cedar are as pleasant as any in the Hawiian Islands. The weather here is often better than in the crater and can provide several days of alternative hiking.

The Hana Coast of Maui is of special interest to hikers looking for balmy oceanside walking with rocky cliffs, breaking waves, and warm waters. Further inland, trails lead through thick jungles to streams, waterfalls, and pools of rare beauty. Nearby campgrounds provide good bases for a leisurely tour of these regions. The lush greenery on this side of Maui does have its price: there is much rain. However, the rain is intermittent and warm.

You may fly into the regions described in this book via the Kahului or Hana airports. Only small planes land at the Hana airport. Rental cars are available at these airports. Hitch-hiking, though illegal, seems to be a popular form of transportation to the hiking areas. The trails on Maui are among the best known in the state, so make reservations well in advance with the appropriate agencies for the use of the cabins described here.

10. Polipoli Loop

3½-hour loop
800 calories; difficulty B
4.9-mile loop
Highest point: 6200 feet
Elevation loss: 900 feet
Maps: Maui 1:62,500
      Kilohana, Lualailua Hills,
      Makena 1:24,000
Division of State Parks
Division of Forestry and Wildlife

The Polipoli Loop in Polipoli State Park is 6,000 feet up the slopes below Haleakala Crater and central to the trail network in the Kula and Kahikinui Forest Reserves. It passes through a forest which provides examples of the varied results of reforestation with trees exotic to Hawaii. The species include Monterey cypress, ash, sugi, pine, red alder, redwood, several varieties of eucalyptus, and many others. Examples have been labeled along the trailside. The Polipoli Loop, through these deep, varied forests, is well maintained and has a gentle grade for easy walking. This loop trail is made up of portions of the Polipoli, Haleakala Ridge, Plum, and Redwood Trails. It serves as an introduction to the area, which at present has more than ten well-marked and well-maintained trails with a total length of over 20 miles. The Division of State Parks has additional trail descriptions.

Redwood forest — Polipoli Loop

Camping for up to one week is allowed in the park with a permit from the Division of State Parks (P.O. Box 1049, Wailuku, Maui, HI 96793). One cabin is available by reservation. The elevation makes the area cold in winter and cool at night even in summer, so dress warmly. This lovely forest is highly vulnerable to fire during dry periods. Drinking water is available at Polipoli campground only.

Route: From Kahului drive on Highway 37 almost 14 miles to the second turnoff left (east) onto Highway 377 (Upper Kula Road) toward Haleakala National Park. Follow Highway 377 about 0.3 miles to the turnoff to the right (southeast) up Waipoli Road (Kaonulu Ranch Road). Waipoli Road is surfaced for 2.7 miles and then dirt and gravel for 5.7 miles. It is rough but usually passable for small cars except after rainstorms. It switchbacks steeply uphill, climbing about 3000 feet and then contours

south. A little less than 3.5 miles after entering the Kula Forest Reserve the road splits, one fork going uphill to Polipoli Hill and the other fork turning downhill (right) to Polipoli Mountain Park and the trailhead 0.2 miles away.

Park at the end of the road and take the Polipoli Trail which starts at the south (downhill end) of the parking lot. The trail begins in a dense stand of Monterey cypress and contours easily to the Haleakala Ridge Trail 0.6 miles south through cypress, cedar, and Monterey pine. The junction of the two trails is at the upper edge of a grassy area. The loop route follows the Haleakala Ridge Trail downhill and right, proceeding through splendid stands of eucalyptus, blackwood, swamp mahogany, and hybrid cypress. About 0.4 miles beyond this junction, a short side trail leads left into a cinder cone with an interesting shelter cave at the bottom.

The Haleakala Ridge Trail then passes

Along the road to Polipoli

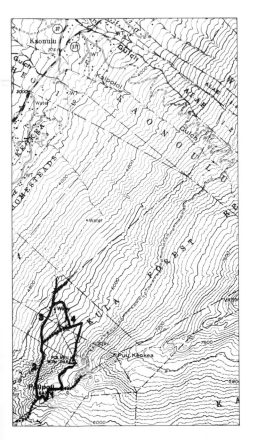

the Plum Trail, which leads off north (right) through cool, dense stands of conifers and past fruit-bearing plum trees. The Polipoli Loop leaves the Haleakala Ridge Trail and follows the Plum Trail from this junction.

About a mile from the junction of the Haleakala Ridge Trail and the Plum Trail, the Tie Trail leads in from uphill (right). It comes down from the Redwood Trail, which returns to the parking area. Those wishing to shorten the hike can follow the Tie Trail. If you proceed along the Plum Trail, 0.6 miles beyond its junction with the Tie Trail, you will reach an old CCC bunkhouse and cabin. Camping here is allowed by permit from the Division of State Parks. Near the cabin, the Plum Trail ends as it meets the Boundary Trail coming in from the left (north) and the Redwood Trail coming in from the right (northeast).

To return to the parking area take the Redwood Trail, which soon turns south-east. The trail proceeds uphill through Mexican pine, tropical ash, Port Orford cedar, and redwood. It is joined by the upper end of the Tie Trail 0.9 miles from the CCC bunkhouse. The Redwood Trail continues uphill, passing a Division of State Parks cabin a couple of hundred yards before reaching the parking area.

11. Sliding Sands-Halemauu

2 days; 9 hours
2500 calories; difficulty C
11.3 miles one way
Highest point: 9800 feet
Elevation loss: 3300 feet
Elevation gain: 1550 feet
Maps: Maui 1:62,500
**   Kilohana, Nahiku, 1:24,000**
Haleakala National Park

Words cannot adequately describe Haleakala Crater. It must be seen. The expanse of lava flows, vents, cones, and fields of volcanic ash resembles the surface of the moon. It is an awesome, other worldly sight. The Sliding Sands-Halemauu route offers an overnight or a hard one-day trip through the crater, giving a good look at a large part of it. Since the exit on Halemauu Trail is several miles away from and lower than the entrance on the Sliding Sands Trail, located at almost 10,000 feet near the top of Haleakala, arrangements must be made to shuttle between the trailheads. The trip can be made in one day by strong hikers but it is more pleasant to take two days. If you plan to stay in one of the cabins in the crater, confirm your plans with Haleakala National Park three months in advance (P.O. Box 369, Makawao, HI 96768). Camping permits for the back-country camping areas are available on a first-come, first-serve basis at the park headquarters.

Hosmer Grove, located down the road about 4 miles from the trailhead, makes a good base camp, if the trail is to be hiked in one day. The grove was planted in 1910 with many varieties of mainland trees. Native birds flit among their branches. A short nature trail leads from the campground through this mainland forest, passing examples of native plants. Water, a picnic shelter, restrooms, and space for tent camping are available, with no permit or reservation required at present.

Since the weather at these high altitudes can suddenly become cold with high winds and rain or snow, it is necessary to take along boots, waterproofs, warm wool clothes, extra clothes, and, if camping, a

Southwest from Ka Moa o Pele

sleeping bag and a waterproof tent. If one is poorly outfitted and facing the uncertainties of weather, it is best to philosophize that the mountain will still be there and descend back down the road to enjoy Maui's balmy beaches.

Route: Drive from Kahului on Highway 37 about 10 miles to the turnoff left (east) onto Highway 377 to Haleakala National Park. Follow Highway 377 about 6.5 miles then turn up Haleakala Crater Road (Highway 378). Follow this slow, switchbacking road about 10 miles to the park boundary. At 0.7 miles beyond the park boundary, you will pass Hosmer Grove and

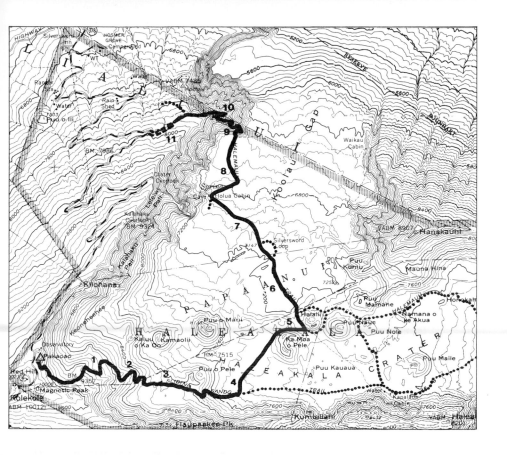

Haleakala Crater — amaumau ferns

shortly thereafter you will reach the park headquarters. Stop at the headquarters for current information regarding camping and hiking. The short turnoff to the exit of the Halemauu Trail is located 4.6 miles past the park boundary. Drive on to the visitor center near the top of Haleakala, 10.6 miles up the road from the park boundary. Day hikers must register for the hike down the Sliding Sands Trail at the box near the Haleakala visitor center. Overnight campers need a permit from the park headquarters. The trailhead is well marked and the trail is easy to follow as it switchbacks down over talus mantled by ash and cinders onto the crater floor. Resist the temptation to cut the switchbacks since this is a discourtesy to others, causes erosion, and is illegal.

From the descending trail there are good views of the whole crater and the rivers of clouds which flow into the crater through Koolau Gap (to the northeast) and Kaupo Gap (to the east). Vegetation is sparse or absent until one reaches the crater floor. Little bracken ferns, pili grass, shrubs, and flowers begin to appear, increasing in numbers as one travels east. As the trail

flattens out it passes a cinder cone, Puu o Pele (Hill of Pele), off to the left (north). The trail then begins another, moderately steep descent to the crater floor beyond Puu o Pele. At the end of this descent and almost at the four-mile point the Sliding Sands Trail is joined by a connecting trail leading northeast a mile and a half across the crater floor to the Halemauu Trail. The Sliding Sands Trail leads straight ahead, east, reaching Kapalaoa Cabin after 1.8 miles and Paliku Cabin after 5.8 miles from this junction.

Take the connecting trail, left (north), toward the left shoulder of Ka Moa o Pele, a red and black cinder cone toward the center of the crater. The trail leads across relatively flat, ash-covered flows of basalt, then climbs up the cinder-covered side of Ka Moa o Pele to a saddle between it and an older cone adjacent to the north. The saddle is one of the best places in the crater for taking pictures of the colorful landscape and impressive cones to the west. Nearby grow fine examples of the silversword. Use care to stay several feet away since their delicate feeder roots lie just below the surrounding cinders.

Silversword

Moonscape

Nene goose

The trail descends to the saddle between Ka Moa o Pele and Halalii cinder cone to the northeast. The trail skirts a small, narrow flow of dark gray basaltic *pahoehoe* (smooth) lava called "Pele's Pig Pen." At Pele's Pig Pen it joins the trail circling Halalii. Here one can go right, circling the cone to its northeast side, or go left, northwest. Take care not to take the trail to Kapalaoa, as it branches to the right (southeast) a short distance beyond Pele's Pig Pen. Either route around Halalii ends up on the Halemauu Trail. Just as the route to the right joins the Halemauu Trail, it passes "the Bottomless Pit," a deep volcanic vent. As Halemauu Trail continues on to the north of Halalii it passes a colorful spatter cone area called "Pele's Paint Pot." The route to the left misses these but saves about half a mile of travel.

Once the Halemauu Trail is reached, follow it west and north across a barren moonscape of ash and lava to Holua cabin, which lies 1.9 miles from the northwest flank of Halalii. Midway to the cabin the trail passes the Silversword Loop. This half-mile loop provides good views of silverswords.

The Halemauu Trail gradually climbs out of the deepest ash as it passes the Silversword Loop and moves onto red, then black lava with firmer footing and increasing vegetation, including kukaenene, pukeiawe, and evening primrose. It slowly descends for a mile before reaching Holua Cabin. The cabin and nearby water tank sit above the trail near the crater wall. A tent camping area (by permit) is located about 200 yards south of the cabin. Open fires are not permitted anywhere in the crater. Be courteous and do not disturb those who have rented the cabins.

From Holua Cabin the trail goes generally north, down the lava, and across a meadow to the switchbacks leading back up the crater wall. From the meadow the trail climbs a twisting, lovely course to gain over a thousand feet to the crater rim. Hikers should be sure to step aside and stand quietly next to the trail to let horses pass by. Along the way one may see a handsome display of the red and green amaumau ferns. At length the top of the wall is reached and the trail climbs gradually through hinahina and other native Hawaiian plants to the start of the road somewhat over a mile away, passing a side trail going downhill to Hosmer Grove along the way.

12. Sliding Sands-Kaupo Gap

2-3 days; 13-14 hours down
5300 calories; difficulty C
17.5 miles one way
Highest point: 9800 feet
Elevation loss: 9500 feet
Maps: Maui 1:62,500
        Kaupo, Kilohana, Nahiku 1:24,000
Haleakala National Park

This is the grand tour of Haleakala Crater, traversing its entire length from west to east and descending through Kaupo Gap to the sea coast: a total drop of almost 10,000 feet in about 18 miles. It has the advantage of being nearly all downhill, but the disadvantage that transportation must be provided at the lower end to avoid a monumental return trip.

Haleakala Crater was formed by two great valleys, Koolau and Kaupo. Erosion caused these to join together and widen at their heads. Subsequent volcanic activity covered the area with lava and cinder cones leaving a barren and beautiful landscape.

The trail starts out at nearly 10,000 feet, where the air is clear and the view immense. A wide-angle lens is useful because of the scale of the scenery. The crater can be very windy, wet, and cold. Therefore, it is necessary to take boots, waterproofs, warm wool clothes, extra clothes, tents, and sleeping bags. The weather is remarkably changeable in the crater. It is possible to suffer from both severe sunburn and hypothermia on the same day. If unprepared, one should avoid this hike.

Two cabins, Kapalaoa and Paliku, are located along this route. If you plan to stay in these you must make reservations three months in advance with Haleakala National Park. Water is usually available at tanks next to the cabins. Camping is not permitted near Kapalaoa, but a tent camping area is located 200 yards from Paliku Cabin. Camping permits for Poliku Campground are available at the park headquarters on a first-come, first-serve basis. To preserve the area, open fires are forbidden.

Route: Drive to Haleakala National Park

West of Kapalaoa Cabin

headquarters. Stop to obtain the latest information regarding conditions and permits. Go 10.5 miles to the visitor center near the top of Haleakala. The trail begins near the center and is well marked as the "Sliding Sands Trail," the only apparent route down the slopes into the crater. Day hikers must sign in.

Follow the Sliding Sands Trail down to Kapalaoa Cabin, located about 5.8 miles from the trailhead and 4.0 miles from Paliku Cabin. If you have arranged to stay overnight at Kapalaoa Cabin instead of proceeding directly to Paliku, it is worthwhile to explore some of the short trails leading north from the cabin to various points of interest. From Kapalaoa Cabin proceed east down the well-marked trail to join the Halemauu Trail. Continue east (right) down the Halemauu Trail, passing

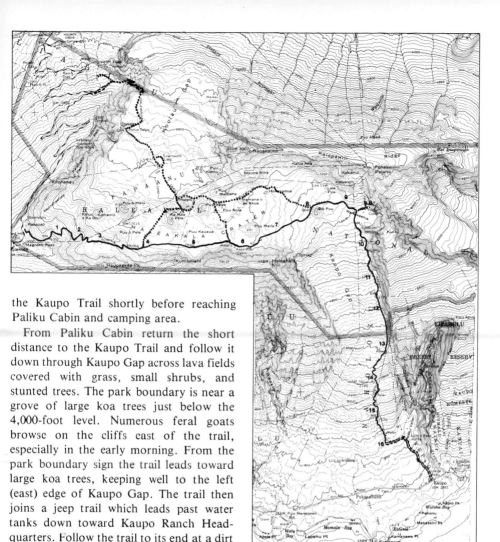

the Kaupo Trail shortly before reaching Paliku Cabin and camping area.

From Paliku Cabin return the short distance to the Kaupo Trail and follow it down through Kaupo Gap across lava fields covered with grass, small shrubs, and stunted trees. The park boundary is near a grove of large koa trees just below the 4,000-foot level. Numerous feral goats browse on the cliffs east of the trail, especially in the early morning. From the park boundary sign the trail leads toward large koa trees, keeping well to the left (east) edge of Kaupo Gap. The trail then joins a jeep trail which leads past water tanks down toward Kaupo Ranch Headquarters. Follow the trail to its end at a dirt road just below the ranch headquarters. This dirt road leads down to the coastal road (Highway 31, the "King's Highway," or the Piilani Highway).

Drivers meeting you at the trail's end must either drive the dry, barren coastal road east from Ulupalakua or drive west from Hana for about 17 miles on the scenic but rough coastal road. The road from Ulupalakua is usually in better condition, closed less often by washouts, and a shorter distance from central Maui than the road from Hana. A good landmark for the turnoff to the side leading up to the trailhead is a picturesque seaside church 0.5 miles east of the turnoff. Kaupo is located just west of the turnoff. Since there is little to amuse those waiting at the trail's end, and the

coastal road to Hana is spectacular, hikers could walk down to the road and along it east about nine miles to the Haleakala National Park's Oheo Campground and the Waimoku Falls area (described in this book).

An alternative to the hike to the seacoast from Poliku Cabin is to hike back up the crater via the Halemauu Trail located on the north side of the crater (described earlier in this book). Holua Cabin is 6.3 miles from Paliku Cabin via this interesting route, which eliminates the difficult problem of arranging transportation from the sea coast.

13. Waimoku Falls (Oheo Gulch)

2 hours up, 1½ hours down
1050 calories; difficulty B
2 miles one way
Highest point: 1000 feet
Elevation gain: 850 feet
Maps: Maui 1:62,500
　　　　Kipahulu 1:24,000
Haleakala National Park

This is an area of swimming holes and waterfalls of remarkable beauty where the ancient Hawaiians lived, fished, farmed, and swam. The pools have long been considered one of the most attractive areas on Maui. The federal government recognized the area's beauty and preserved it as a part of Haleakala National Park. The inevitable result of such fame and recognition is that the lovely pools near the road can be crowded. Fortunately, other attractive areas exist upstream. The lack of crowds there reflects a natural law first formulated by Professor Joel Hildebrand. According to Hildebrand's Law the number of people in a wilderness area diminishes in proportion to the square of the distance and the cube of the elevation from the nearest road. Thus, the upper areas are reserved for those willing to walk. The trail to the upper areas leads to a viewpoint overlooking Makahiku Falls and to Waimoku Falls farther up the valley.

Route: From Hana, on the east end of Maui, follow Highway 31 southwest 10 miles to a small bridge crossing Oheo Gulch. A parking area is located less than a quarter of a mile past the bridge. A short, well-maintained trail parallels the southwest side of the stream, providing good views of the pools below the bridge. Avoid viewing from the narrow, heavily traveled bridge. The pools below the bridge provide good swimming, though there is the possibility of flash floods. The ocean currents are dangerous and local sharks are reputed to have developed a taste for warm meat. The Waimoku Falls Trail begins across the road from the parking area. Proceed directly up the hillside, following the obvious trail

Waimoku Falls Trail

which roughly parallels the course of Oheo Stream. The track forks about 800 paces from its begining; the right fork goes 50 paces to the brink of a cliff overlooking Makahiku Falls. After regaining the main trail follow it up through pasture toward the head of the valley. There the trail drops steeply down a bank, through guava, mango, and Christmas-berry, to reach Palikea Stream. The trail crosses the stream just above a small pool into which two small waterfalls plunge.

The trail then climbs the bank of Palikea Stream, leads through guava and thickets of bamboo, past overgrown taro patches, over small boardwalks, and through a nar-

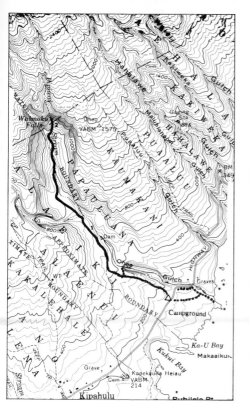

row corridor in a final thicket of bamboo. On the far side of the corridor the trail comes to Pipiwai Stream and turns left. It then closely follows the bank of the stream about 300 paces to its confluence with another stream from the left. Shortly after the confluence, the trail crosses the left-hand stream and proceeds up the right-hand stream to Waimoku Falls, about 250 paces beyond the confluence. Avoid swimming in or crossing these streams during high water. If the water level rises, get out fast; upstream rains can create dangerous flashfloods.

The national park's Oheo Campground is located along a dirt road leading a half mile seaward from the parking area. This waterless campground is quite large and sits on a spectacular, mosquito-free location above Kukui Bay. The closest supply of potable water is in Hana. Waianapanapa State Park, described under the Hana-Waianapanapa Coastal Trail, is also a good location for tent camping (by permit). Make reservations months in advance to use the cabins in the state park.

Oheo Gulch — falls and plunge pool

14. Hana-Waianapanapa Coastal Trail

2 hours in, 2 hours out
700 calories; difficulty B
3 miles one way
Highest point: 40 feet
Elevation gain: 50 feet
Maps: Maui 1:62,500
Hana 1:24,000
Division of State Parks

Waianapanapa State Park is set in a wooded location between Hana airport and the small community of Hana beside two pebbly, little beaches on Pailoa Bay. Reservations for the rental cabins at the campground must be made months in advance. Picnic tables, showers, tent sites, and restroom facilities are available.

The coastal trail next to the campground is a jewel among coastal trails in the state. It parallels the sea along small lava cliffs formed by the action of the waves on recent flows and is bounded inland by a dense forest of hala trees. The play of light in the early morning or late evening on the dark, textured lava and the light surf makes the area especially suited for black and white photography. At midday the light is flat and the trail can be too warm, with little shade and no potable water.

In addition to its beauty, the trail has historic interest since it follows the ancient Hawaiian "King's Highway" paralleling Maui's seacoast. Smooth, water-worn stepping stones placed on the jagged lava to soften the trail for the feet of travelers mark this ancient Hawaiian trail. The kings of the island and their retainers following the trail would come to collect taxes from the various districts. The stones are so old that rain water has eroded many of them. Not far from the park the trail passes an ancient *heiau* (temple) and several building foundations. The remarkable flower called beach naupaka flourishes along the trail. Its blossoms appear to have but half a flower; a related species with only half a flower is found in the mountains. This peculiarity has given rise to many legends. One relates that the gods, tiring of the quarrels of two

Naupaka

lovers, turned them into these distinctive flowers and condemned them to live apart, one in the mountains and one by the sea.

Route: Coming from the north on the Hana Highway (360), go 0.6 miles past the Hana Airport turnoff to the Waianapanapa Campground turnoff on the left (seaward). Proceed down this narrow, paved, two-lane road to the campground. The trail can be joined at any point between the campground and the sea since it extends along the coast in both directions. The portion going east toward Hana is the longer and more interesting, first passing a blowhole and then the ruins of a *heiau*. The trail ends at Kainalimu Bay.

The portion of the trail west of the campground goes by two small, pleasant beaches, Pailoa and Keawaiki, and then leads on to the rough lava country close to the airport. The terrain becomes less interesting after leaving the beaches and progressively more rugged.

Waianapanapa Cave is a nearby feature of historic interest, reached by a short trail just west of the campground. Here a queen of Maui sought refuge from victorious enemies by swimming underwater to a hidden portion of the cave. To her misfortune, a faint trail of blood revealed the hiding place to her pursuers, who killed her.

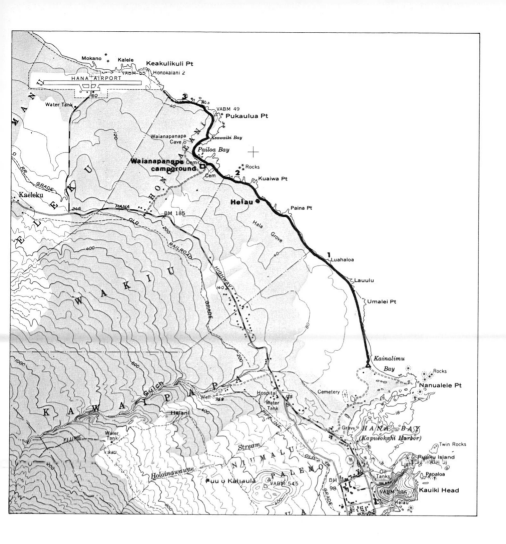

The "King's Highway"

15. Keanae Arboretum

1 hour in, 3/4 hours out
400 calories; difficulty A
1.5 miles one way
Highest point: 500 feet
Elevation gain: 300 feet
Maps: Maui 1:62,500
         Keanae 1:24,000
Division of Forestry and Wildlife

Taro was the most important food crop of the original Hawaiians. It is immensely productive and almost immune to the depredations of insects and animals because of calcium oxalate crystals in it which sting predators. Thorough cooking destroys the crystals and makes taro safe to eat. Poi, the staple of the original Hawaiians' diet, is made from taro roots. The young leaves of the plant provided the substance of several nourishing dishes. Taro is generally grown in paddies washed by fresh-flowing streams.

Besides going through attractive scenery, the Keanae Arboretum Trail offers interesting examples of taro cultivation. The trail skirts along paddies in Keanae Arboretum containing a variety of species. Other areas display examples of bananas and sugar cane cultivated by the ancient Hawaiians. The trail passes beyond Keanae Arboretum, crosses Pokakaekane Stream and follows Kuo Stream up into native lowland rain forest.

Route: Drive east on Highway 360 from Kahului approximately 47 miles to a sharp turn in the road just after the Keanae YMCA Camp and just before the turnoff to Keanae. Parking is available next to a large sign indicating Keanae Arboretum. A gate blocks traffic down the dirt road to the arboretum. Pass through this gate on foot and continue a short distance on the dirt road to a second gate, which leads to the arboretum itself. In the arboretum the trail passes a small swimming hole in Piinaau Stream and irrigated taro patches. It continues up Piinaau Stream, passes out of the arboretum area, crosses small Pokakaekane Stream, and turns up at Kuo Stream. The

Pool on Piinaau Stream

trail follows Kuo Stream closely and crosses it frequently until the trail disappears in the rain forest after about 0.5 miles. Along the way the damp soil and rotting logs support profusions of strangely colored mushrooms of many varieties.

On the return trip it is worth making a side visit down to Piinaau Stream. The best access is where the trail crosses Pokakaekane Stream. From the crossing go 50 yards downstream to the confluence with Piinaau Stream. At the confluence it becomes apparent that a narrow faultline has allowed Piinaau Stream to form a series of small waterfalls and beautiful, deep pools. One that is good for swimming is just a few yards upstream from the confluence. Beware of flash flooding. The best overnight tent camping in the area (by permit) is located at Waianapanapa State Park near Hana (described under the Hana-Waianapanapa Coastal Trail). To use the cabins at the park, make reservations months in advance.

Taro patches

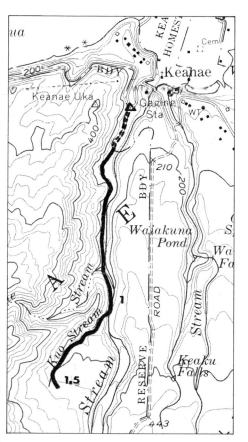

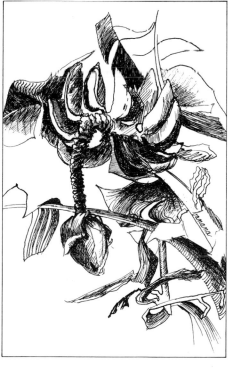

16. Waikamoi Ridge Loop

1/2 hour up, 1/4 hour down
150 calories; difficulty A
1.0 mile loop
Highest point: 800 feet
Elevation gain: 200 feet
Maps: Maui 1:62,500
       Keanae 1:24,000
Division of Forestry and Wildlife

The Waikamoi Ridge Loop Trail is the shortest and easiest trail on Maui described in this book. It is well maintained and easy to follow, with an even grade and surface. It leads up a heavily wooded slope to a grassy area with a small, open shelter and picnic tables. The forest through which it passes is made up of plants introduced to Hawaii in the last 100 years, including bamboo and several varieties of large eucalyptus trees, along with some handsome native ferns and trees. The trail and picnic site have no water or restroom facilities. Camping is not permitted.

Route: Drive from Kahului 41 miles on Highway 360 to 3.5 miles past Kailua. The trailhead is on the south (uphill) side of the road and is well marked by a pipe fence and a sign. There is ample room for parking. A picnic shelter is located in a stand of large eucalyptus near the trailhead. The trail leads uphill to the south from the trailhead and picnic shelter through a stand of large eucalyptus, hand-planted about 50 years ago. Many of the trees and shrubs along the trail are labelled for identification. A stone bench is located half-way up the trail as a rest point, providing a view of a nearby forested valley. As the trail gains the ridgeline, the return leg of the loop heads downhill to the left. Proceed right, to the main trail's end at a hilltop picnic site a few minutes past the bench.

The shelter at the end of the trail, bordered by scattered flowers and surrounded by a lawn, is an admirable picnic spot for a family. There is ample room for small children to romp under the watchful eyes of their parents. The view of the surrounding hills, though not breathtaking, is

Eucalyptus forest

pleasant. Exposed to the breeze and in a sunny clearing, the area is nearly free of mosquitoes.

Since the trail goes through a damp area with a northern exposure, there is sometimes a profusion of colorful mushrooms sprouting from fallen logs and forest debris along the route. Tent camping is available by permit at Waianapanapa State Park, close to Hana. Directions are given under the Hana-Waianapanapa Coastal Trail. To use the cabins there, make reservations months in advance.

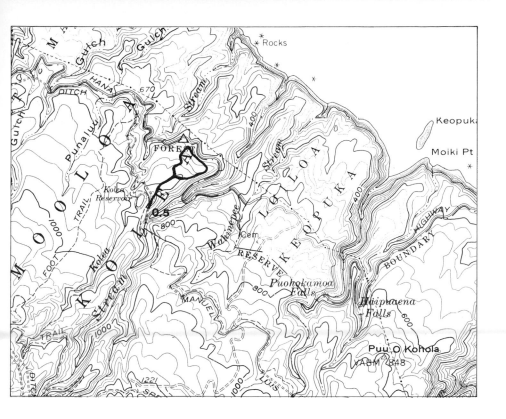

Picnic area

Islands of Lanai and Molokai

Lanai provides one of the clearest examples of early conservation efforts designed to overcome the damage of past overgrazing. At one time, Lanai supported a fairly large population and was covered with native vegetation. Importation of cattle and goats a century ago made the island virtually a desert. Later owners of Lanai, including most recently Castle and Cooke, have made commendable efforts to halt the erosion and destruction of the island's watershed. Wild cattle and goats were brought under control. Exotic trees and grasses were planted to hold the soil. Vigorous stands of eucalyptus, tall rows of Norfolk Island pine, and a gradually advancing forest illustrate the long-term success of the policy. More recently, the corporation has generously placed a portion of the island containing rare, native dryland forest under a conservation easement to the Nature Conservancy of Hawaii.

Koele Company maintains the only campground on the island of Lanai, at Hulopoe Beach, a beach area on the south side of the island close to Manele Bay. Persons wishing to camp there should contact Koele Company (address in introduction) and make arrangements for their stay. Stays are limited to one week and require a small fee. A rental car is needed to reach the camp. Since water sources are few and fire danger can be great, camping is not permitted on the other areas of the island. Hiking, on a day basis, is limited to those who are at the camping area or staying at one of the hotels on the island.

Lanai City, the only town, is located in the center of the island. There are daily meals and a small number of rooms available at Lanai Hotel, a most charming and authentic part of old Hawaii. The Lodge at Koele north of Lanai City provides modern accommodations.

Four trails on Lanai are described. Three center around its gorges and wooded areas: the Kaiholena Gulch Loop, Munro, and North Hauola Trails. The fourth trail is a hike along isolated Polihua Beach. Four-wheel-drive vehicles are necessary to reach the Polihua Beach and North Hauola Trails. Check with your hosts for current information on transportation and hiking.

Three trails are described on Molokai. The Halawa Trail leads through a verdant valley to a large waterfall and pool. The Kalaupapa Trail, descending the precipitous face of a great scarp, provides impressive views of the North Coast. The Kalaupapa trailhead is located close to isolated Paalau State Park. A short trail leads from the park campground to nearby Phallic Rock.

The trail to the Nature Conservancy Preserve in the Pepeopae Bog is located in the forest areas above the North Coast. It is

The destroyer

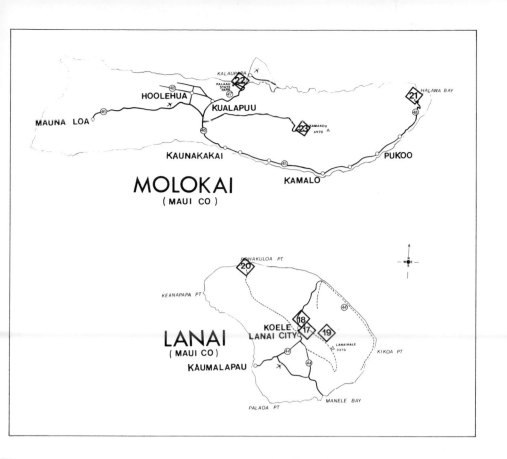

East Lanai

Moaula Falls — Halawa Valley

North Coast — Molokai

accessible via four-wheel-drive Molokai Forest Reserve road leading in from the west off Highway 46. Along the way the road passes the Sandalwood Pit and a grand view of the Waikolu Valley.

Several reasonable hotels in Kaunakakai, on the southern coast, provide lodging and food. The destination resort in the westernmost part of Molokai is located on one of the most delightful beaches in Hawaii. Visitor transportation around the island of Molokai is generally by rental car or hitch-hiking (though illegal). There is no public transportation.

Panini Cactus

17. Kaiholena Gulch Loop

4-hour loop
1100 calories; difficulty B
4-mile loop
Highest point: 2800 feet
Elevation gain: 1050 feet
Map: Lanai 1:62,500
Koele Company

The reforested area of Lanai is perhaps the best example in the Hawaiian Islands of the success of carefully planned conservation after the ravages of overgrazing in the late 1800's and early 1900's. The trail follows a ridge which eventually leads to Lanaihale, the highest point on the island. Along the way it passes planted ironwood, eucalyptus, and Norfolk Island pine, all exotic to Hawaii. Just as planned many years ago, these plantings now steadily wring water directly from mists borne on the trade winds. As the mists pass over the high ridges, tiny water droplets accumulate on leaves and needles until large drops form and finally fall to earth. This process is called "fog drip" and steadily accumulates great quantities of water for the island.

Route: Before starting, check with Koele Company to find out about possible shotgun hunters in the area. From the post office in Lanai City, drive or walk along Keomoku Road (Highway 44) north to the pineapple fields. There the road turns right (easterly) and travels beside the golf course. Beyond the golf course the highway turns left (northerly). Just as it turns, a secondary road comes in from the right. Follow the secondary road to the right for about 200 paces south toward Lanai City to where a side road enters from the left (east). Proceed up this side road on the north side of grass-filled Kaiholena Gulch past several possible turnoffs until you reach a grove of over a hundred large Norfolk Island pines. About a third of the way up the grove, park and walk 40 paces through the grove to its other side.

The Kaiholena Gulch Loop Trail goes directly up to a pair of power poles about

Beginning of the Kaiholena Gulch Loop

150 paces away on the hill. The trail climbs sharply to the pair of power poles, passes between them, and follows under the powerlines for about 30 paces. It then angles right, uphill into the forest and continues up the ridgeline beside a row of Norfolk Island pines. The trail is indistinct, but follow the ridge and the pines and you will not go far wrong. Stay on the highest part of the ridge all the way to its intersection with the Munro Trail (a jeep road and trail described later in this book).

The Kaiholena Gulch Loop Trail first passes through planted stands of ironwood, eucalyptus, and Norfolk Island pine. Higher up it passes through underbrush of native staghorn fern, ohia lehua, ti plants, tree ferns, and ieie, a native screw pine. The ridge, swept steadily by the trade winds offers good views of the Islands of Lanai, Molokai, and the west half of Maui.

The intersection with the Munro Trail is at the junction of the ridge which the Kaiholena Gulch Loop follows and the one which the Munro Trail follows, about a mile from the loop's start. Each ridge is marked by a single row of Norfolk Island pines along its crest. Turn right (southeast) onto the Munro Trail. After 0.3 miles it starts up a small rise and then descends to a

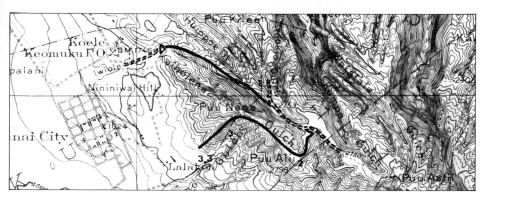

Albezzia and eucalyptus trees below reflector

narrow ridge through young sugi and Norfolk Island pine. Shortly after the climb and
the descent to the narrow ridge, the trail
passes a short road on the right which leads
to a rain gauge and the remnants of a
building. Turn off here to begin the route
back down the southwest side of Kaiholena
Gulch.

The return trail is not distinct and dead
reckoning must be resorted to at times.
Start in the grass and staghorn ferns near
the rain gauge and choose one of the several
faint trails leading along the ridge to an apparently isolated knoll 400 yards to the
southwest. Head for the high point of this
knoll, where the trail becomes more
distinct. The trail turns sharply to the right

(northwest) at the knoll, follows the
ridgeline down gently for about 0.4 miles,
and then begins a short, steep, eroded
descent. The trail continues down the
ridgetop to a grove of eucalyptus. A little
farther, at another grove of eucalyptus the
trail turns down a side ridge which comes in
from the left at a 90-degree angle. Be sure
to go all the way to the junction of the side
ridge and the main ridge before making the
turn. Follow the side ridge through the
brush and over badly eroded land to a large
communications reflector. Continue past
the reflector to the pineapple fields below to
return to Lanai City, visible in the distance,
or follow the pineapple fields northwest to
the start of the trail.

18. Munro Trail

7 hours one way
2750 calories; difficulty C
8.5 miles one way
Highest point: 3370 feet
Elevation gain: 1400 feet
Map: Lanai 1:62,500
Koele Company

The Munro Trail is named after George Munro, the man responsible for carrying out the reforestation of the Island of Lanai in the early part of this century. Originally, it was merely an access trail into the forest and watershed areas of Lanai; now it is a rough jeep road. It serves as an easy-to-follow foot trail from the drier areas of the island through the heart of the forest and over the highest point on Lanai, Lanaihale, at 3,370 feet. On a clear day it provides fine views of the Islands of Molokai, Maui, Hawaii, Kahoolawe, and even Oahu.

Route: Drive north from Lanai City along Keomoku Road (Highway 44) about 1.5 miles to the entrance of the Munro Trail, located just before the top of a low pass and marked by a sign. The Munro Trail soon passes a side road from the Lanai Cemetery, located on the right. Go straight ahead. You may leave your car at any point and walk or, if conditions permit, drive along the trail. No drinking water is available. The trail contours through grassland and in and out of gullies reforested with eucalyptus, until it nears Maunalei Gulch, where it begins a long uphill climb. A short side road to the left near the start of the uphill climb leads to a good view of Maunalei Gulch. About 3 miles from the start, the trail passes Hookio Gulch, a branch of Maunalei Gulch. The ridge between the gulches was the stronghold of fleeing Lanai Islanders who were attacked by an army from the Island of Hawaii 200 years ago. The defenders were reduced by starvation and then massacred.

About 3.5 miles along the Munro Trail, the initial leg of the Kaiholena Gulch Loop

A woodland orchid (blue spathoglottis)

(described earlier in this book) joins the Munro Trail. The return leg of the Kaiholena Gulch Loop leads off toward Lanai City at a viewpoint another half-mile along the Munro Trail. The Munro Trail continues to the top of Lanaihale, a good turnaround point, then proceeds down to the south of the island leading into the upper fields above the main pineapple plantations. From there you may proceed along the dirt roads leading back through the pineapple fields to Lanai City, about four miles away from the trail's end at the pineapple fields.

Before starting, check with Koele Company to find out about hunters in the area.

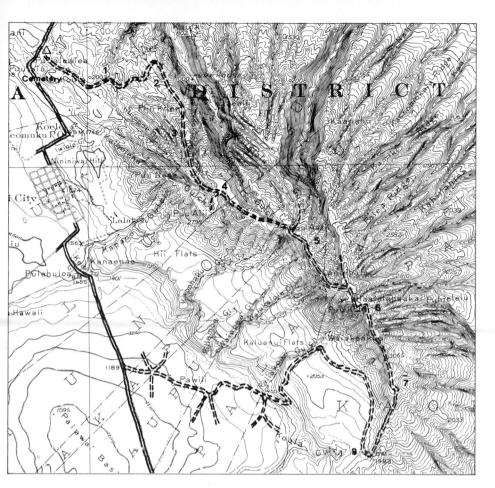

Norfolk Island pines at junction of Munro and Kaiholena Gulch Trails

19. North Hauola

2¾ hours up; 1½ hours down
800 calories; difficulty C
2 miles one way
Highest point: 3200 feet
Elevation gain: 1700 feet
Map: Lanai 1:62,500
Koele Company

Hauola and Maunalei Gulches are spectacular but little-known valleys on the Island of Lanai. Both are over 1500 feet deep and drop so steeply that you must creep up to their very edges to get a good view. A steady blast of wind welling up from the bottom of the canyon meets you as you peer over the edge of Hauola Gulch. Looking into such a precipice in the rushing wind is an exhilarating and somewhat terrifying experience. On a good day the Islands of Molokai, Maui, and Kahoolawe are clearly visible from this side of Lanai. The solitude is as complete as anywhere in the Hawaiian Islands. The heavy overgrowth may make route-finding very difficult. Therefore, special care must be taken to know exactly where you are and have been at all times.

Route: Before starting, check with Koele Company to find out if deer hunters will be in the area. Drive north from Lanai City along Keomoku Road (Highway 44) about 1.5 miles to the entrance of the Munro Trail, located just before the top of a low pass and marked by a sign. The Munro Trail soon passes a road from the Lanai Cemetery, located on the right. After the cemetery turnoff the Munro Trail becomes an infrequently travelled jeep road, impassable in wet weather. The trail contours along the hillside and through gulches up into the forest area, climbing steeply along the west side of Maunalei Gulch and its tributary, Hookio Gulch. The trail reaches a relatively straight stretch about a mile after completing this steep climb. At the end of this straight stretch, it veers left and begins side-hilling up a steep hill to gain about 200 feet of elevation. Immediately after the climb it turns southeast to follow a flatter area for 50 yards. It then climbs for about 50 yards to a slight dip in the road after which it continues up the hill. This dip is occupied by a peculiar, permanent mud puddle, caused by a nearby Norfolk Island pine, which sweeps the moisture from the air, creating a stationary "rain cloud" over this small area. At this mud puddle, there should be a sign on the left (northeast) side of the road marking the start of the North Hauola Trail.

A rain gauge is located a few yards from the trailhead. Park here and follow the steep, rutted trail down through heavy ferns. The trail, which may be obscured by overgrowth, soon begins to lead north, following down the crest of a ridge topped by a row of Norfolk Island pines. About 45 minutes from the start, the trail reaches the

Hauola Gulch

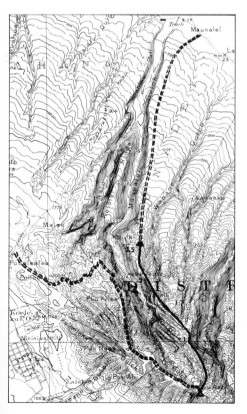

edge of Hauola Gulch, providing an excellent view of this deep canyon. The trail contours down the ridge along the west side of Hauola Gulch, then descends steeply onto a small, grassy swale next to a grove of eucalyptus trees. From this swale, the main trail climbs over a small, barren knoll.

Go into the eucalyptus grove instead of following the main trail, which will shortly end near a fenced square of land used to test overgrazing by goats. Proceed downhill along the floor of the grove for about 300 yards. A faint trail, overgrown by guava trees and underbrush, leads through the eucalyptus grove. The trail will most likely be impossible to find or to follow exactly and you will likely end up bushwacking. The route passes the ruins of a small wooden cowboy hut used many years ago when Lanai was a ranch.

Fifty yards beyond the hut, the route passes out of the grove and skirts up the right hand side of the gully onto the crest of the ridge. Follow this route down the crest for about 0.7 miles, without straying far from the gully, until the ridge ends at Maunalei Gulch near the remnants of an old fence line. From here no trail exists, but since the country is open, it is not difficult to follow along the east ridge of Maunalei Gulch down to a four-wheel-drive track leading to Keomoku Road.

The trail can be approached from below and hiked in reverse by taking Keomoku Road from Lanai City down to the northeast coast of Lanai. Within 0.5 miles after the road completes its descent to the coast, it passes about five houses and a dirt road which enters from the right (south). This is the Koolanai Jeep Trail. Follow this jeep trail for about 4.0 miles to its end. From there walk uphill about 600 yards alongside Maunalei Gulch to the remnants of an old fence line. Just beyond it the faint remnants of the trail to Hauola Gulch lead left, up the near (north) side of a 150-foot-deep gully. The trail is not maintained and may be quite difficult to follow. The route is uphill along the crest of the ridge and close to the gully. Refer to the directions given for the upper approach.

20. Polihua Beach
2 hours in, 2 hours out
560 calories; difficulty A
2 miles one way
Highest point: 20 feet
Elevation gain: 20 feet
Map: Lanai 1:62,500
Koele Company

This easy hike offers beachcoming in the Hawaiian Islands at its best. Innumerable tiny seashells litter the beach and glass balls sometimes wash ashore in large numbers along with other treasures. The Island of Molokai lying only a few miles away across Kalohi Channel is clearly visible during the entire length of the hike. On a weekday this long, wide beach is usually totally deserted, leaving you to beachcomb successfully or contemplate in solitude. Access to the Polihua end of the beach is only by jeep or by foot. The jeep trail is quite steep and rough. There is no particular trail along the beach, but the going is easy between the ocean and the brush-covered lava. Distance is arbitrary.

It is possible to walk as far as the east end of the beach and Highway 44 (Keomuku Road) 8 miles away. This would be a waterless all-day trip and arrangements for a return ride are recommended. The east end of the beach may be reached by a short dirt road which leaves west from Highway 44 just as the highway ends its descent from the interior of the island and turns east down to the shore. A jeep is not required for access via Highway 44, but that route is less interesting.

Route: Start on the north side of Lanai City, where Fraser Avenue enters the pineapple fields. Take the wide, dirt roads across these fields to their northwestern end. Note that the roads in the fields are either 24-foot main roads or 12-foot feeder roads and are subject to being rerouted. About 3.5 miles after entering the pineapple fields, the road leaves the fields and enters fairly flat land covered with high grass. Here a signpost may exist pointing to

Along the road to Polihua

Keoneheehee. Farther along, other signposts may point out Kahue Road, Lapaiki Road, and Awalua Road. Stay on the main road leading northwest to Polihua. About 1.5 miles after the turnoff to Awalua Road, Kaena Road enters from the left and Polihua Road begins to descend steeply over a rough surface. Along the way the road passes extremely eroded areas where rocks of bizarre shapes and colors are exposed. Before the introduction of grazing animals in the 1800's, these same lands had deep soil and native dry land forests.

About 4 miles past Kaena Road turnoff, Polihua Road reaches the beach and branches right and left. Either turnoff ends shortly at the beach. The hike begins at the end of the right-hand branch. There is no particular trail; simply follow the beach as far as you choose. The 2.0 mile point offers a good view of one of the first shipwrecks along the beach. Carry extra liquid, as the trip can be hot and there is no drinking water available. Jeep breakdowns are possible and there is virtually no traffic along Polihua Road. Carry appropriate supplies

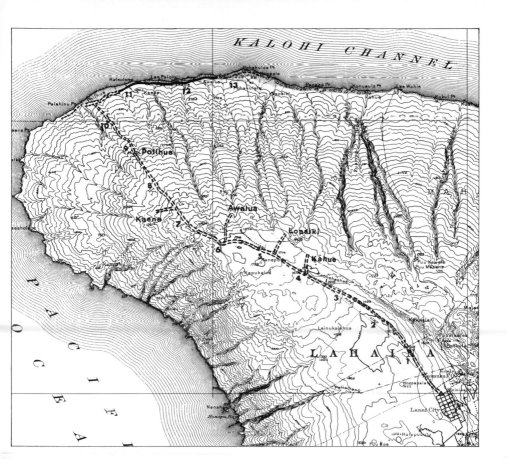

and leave word of your route just in case. The left-hand road leads to the west end of the beach. Not far from the road, the beach ends at rough lava which meets the sea. Since the lava makes for slow, difficult hiking and there is little to see, the route going east is preferable.

Before starting, check with Koele Company to find out about hunters in the area.

Polihua Beach

21. Halawa Valley

2 hours in, 2 hours out
800 calories; difficulty B
2½ miles one way
Highest point: 300 feet
Elevation gain: 250 feet
Maps: Molokai 1:62,500
        Halawa 1:24,000
Customary route over private land

The Halawa Valley is the only one of the four large valleys on the North Shore of Molokai which is accessible by car. The other valleys, Waikolu, Pelekunu, and Wailau, can be reached only with some difficulty on foot or by sea. Waikolu is in a watershed closed to the public, though it could otherwise be reached by trail from Kalaupapa. The trail over the mountains to Wailau presents so many difficulties that it should be attempted only together with people familiar with the area. No trail leads into Pelekunu. The easiest way to reach Wailau and Pelekunu is by sea during the summer.

The Halawa Valley was formerly the home of numerous families subsisting on taro farming and fishing. The last of the taro farming was finished off by the 1946 tidal wave. Now, only a few people live in the valley, which is mostly privately owned.

There are two sets of waterfalls at the end of the valley: Moaula Falls and Hipuapua Falls. Moaula Falls consists of an upper and a lower falls with a large pool at the base of the lower. Hipuapua Falls is a single waterfall with a dumbbell-shaped pool at its base. After heavy rain more falls appear, the water turns reddish-brown, and fording Halawa Stream can become impossible. The pool under Moaula Falls is large enough for enjoyable swimming, with many rocks on which sun-worshippers may bask.

Route: Follow Highway 40/450 to the extreme east end of the island and down the paved road descending into the Halawa Valley.

When the road reaches the valley floor a narrow side road leaves it sharply to the left near a small church. The main road pro-

Upper Moaula Falls

ceeds on to the county park and the beach. There are no overnight facilities at the park. The left-hand road ends at the head of the trail up to Moaula Falls. This narrow half-mile-long road has no room for parking. Park by the main road across from the beginning of the side road and walk to the end of the side road. About 150 yards beyond is a 4-foot gap in the stone fence which parallels the trail. While the main path proceeds straight ahead, another trail turns sharply to the right down to the stream. The usual route to the falls is the path leading down to the stream which can

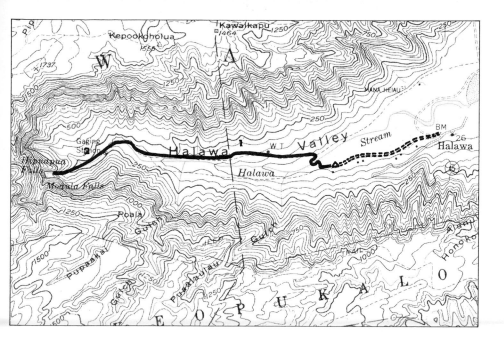

Kukui Nut

be waded across if the water level is safe.

Flooding may obliterate the trail near the stream and change the crossing point. The uncertain route from the opposite bank leads across the low-lying areas and then up through mango trees and brush on the hillside beyond. The distinct trail on the north side of the valley is about fifty feet in elevation above the valley floor and parallels the stream. This well-defined trail leads upstream through taro patches overgrown with guava. Old stone walls and a water pipe parallel the trail for much of its length. About 2.0 miles from the ford, the trail crosses Hipuapua Stream, branching up northwest from Halawa Stream.

About 75 yards after this crossing, the trail forks, with the right-hand trail going steeply uphill toward the upper pool of Moaula Falls. It is hazardous, difficult to follow, and not particularly rewarding. The left-hand trail ends at the lower pool, which is 100 yards past the fork. On the return trip Hipuapua Falls can be reached in about 20 minutes by strenuous rock hopping and clambering up the bed of Hipuapua Stream. There is no trail. The pool at its base is neither as big nor as suitable for swimming as the lower pool at Moaula Falls. However, it is interesting because of its peculiar dumbbell shape formed by a second waterfall which appears only in wet weather. Respect the usual admonitions about the dangers of falling on slippery, rounded stream rocks. Beware of falling rock in the waterfalls.

22. Kalaupapa

1½ hours down, 2½ hours up
1600 calories; difficulty B
2 miles one way
Highest point: 1600 feet
Elevation loss: 1600 feet
Maps: Molokai 1:62,500
      Kaunakakai 1:24,000
State Department of Health

The volcanic Kalaupapa Peninsula was formed long after the rest of the Island of Molokai. Jutting out of the otherwise precipitous North Coast of the island, the peninsula is nearly flat except for small Kauhako Crater toward its central portion. The whole peninsula was set aside in the last century for those afflicted with Hansen's Disease (leprosy). With the onset of effective drug therapy, isolation of patients is no longer necessary. As a result, the number of inhabitants of the peninsula steadily diminishes as the patients leave or die.

Though no longer required to stay at Kalaupapa, many patients consider it their home and have chosen to remain in this beautiful area. They enjoy a lifestyle that is even more tranquil than elsewhere in the islands and are most hospitable to visitors. Permission must be obtained to visit Kalaupapa by contacting the State Department of Health. It is best to arrange an escorted tour through Damien Tours (telephone 1-808-567-6171) which will obtain the necessary permission and charges a reasonable fee for an informative tour of the peninsula.

The peninsula may be reached by small plane or by the trail described in this book. The present trail was reputedly built in the early 1900's by a member of the Joao family of Molokai. For many years it was the main route in and out of Kalaupapa, providing access for the mules bringing provisions. It now provides a scenic path for a day hike down the precipitous north cliffs of Molokai to the settlement. It was not the same trail used by Father Damien, the famous priest who aided the people of the settlement in the early years. That trail was

Kalaupapa Peninsula

probably down the steep cliffs farther to the east. Looking at these cliffs, you realize that not the least of the courageous acts of this remarkable man was simply climbing into and out of the settlement.

Route: From the Molokai airport, take Highway 46/460 to the junction with Highway 47/470. Turn left onto Highway 47/470 and follow it to the end at Palaau State Park. The park has restrooms, water, and numerous tent campsites in a dense ironwood grove. Permits for overnight camping must be obtained in advance from the Division of State Parks on Maui. At the end of the road in the park, a trail leads to Phallic Rock, a considerable rock formation 400 yards away.

To reach the trailhead, drive out of the park to the first turnoff on the left. This is a short dirt road leading down to the rim of the cliff above Kalaupapa. The trail starts just east of a communications facility at the end of the road. Even though the terrain is steep, the trail is wide. Follow the trail down to the base of the cliff and then along the seacoast to the start of the road to the settlement, where you should be met by your guide. Children under 18 are not permitted in the settlement. Overnight lodgings are unavailable, except at the invitation of the patients.

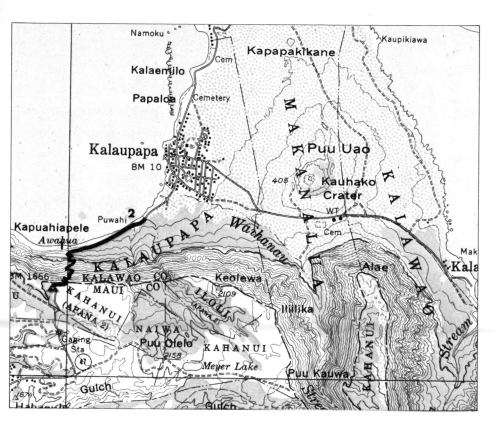

Molokai's North Shore

23. Pepeopae

¾ hours up, ½ hour down
250 calories; difficulty A
0.7 miles one way
Highest point: 4150 feet
Elevation gain: 300 feet
Maps: Molokai 1:62,500
**   Kamalo 1:24,000**
Division of Forestry and Wildlife
The Nature Conservancy of Hawaii

The Pepeopae Bog in the Kamakou Preserve is probably the oldest in Hawaii, containing an irreplaceable remnant of nature as it was before the arrival of man. The Nature Conservancy protects this extraordinary ecosystem today. A narrow boardwalk, constructed by volunteers, leads through the bog to a lookout platform near its high point. The boardwalk protects the bog and saves the hiker from the muddy slog characteristic of wet Hawaiian trails. Use seed-free footwear with good traction. To learn more about the preserve contact the Nature Conservancy of Hawaii: 1116 Smith Street, Suite 201, Honolulu, Hawaii 96817; (808) 537-4508.

Only a four-wheel-drive vehicle can make the ¾ to 1-hour-drive on the rough and sometimes confusing dirt road to the trailhead. Do not even think of taking a passenger car. Although no permit is required, contact the preserve manager for updated information on the condition of the road: P.O. Box 40, Kualapuu, Molokai, HI 96754; (808) 567-6680. It may be closed.

Route: From the west side of Kaunakakai, take Highway 460 westerly. At approximately 3.6 miles turn right (east) onto Molokai Forest Reserve Road, just before coming to a concrete bridge over a dry ravine. Follow the road generally east, as it climbs past former pineapple fields and through lowland covered with imported eucalyptus, silk oak, Cook Island pine and Monterey Cypress. Keep to the main road and ignore numerous turnoffs. The road reaches the Forest Reserve boundary at 5.3 miles from Highway 460 and then soon passes buildings used by Conservancy volunteers. Surrounding areas were reforested

Pepeopae Bog

in the thirties with exotic species. Migratory birds from as far as Alaska may be seen among the thickets.

The road passes a water reservoir at 6.5 miles, skirts Lua Moku Iliahi (the sandalwood measuring pit) at 8.4 miles, and reaches Waikolu Lookout and picnic area at 9.3 miles for an awesome view of the deep valley and its high waterfalls. The road enters the Preserve shortly after passing the

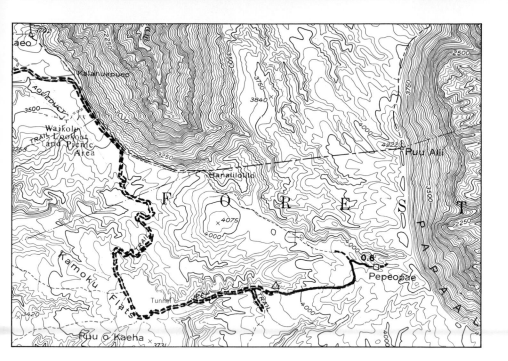

picnic area. Sign in at the box at the entrance. At 9.45 miles the muddy, brushed-over Hanalilolilo Trail enters the road from the left (north). From here the road winds south, crossing over three gulches. Ignore turnoffs to the right, but take the turnoff left at 10.9 miles, which may be signed "Puu Kolekole." At 11.5 milesa left fork in the road leads to the trailhead in 100 yards.

The boardwalk from the trailhead leads gradually uphill into the rain forest. Remain on the boardwalk at all times in this fragile landscape. After about half a mile the trail reaches the cloud-draped bog, with its mosses, sedges, native violets, ancient knee-high ohia lehua trees and lichens strangely reminiscent of Lapland. The outcome of millions of years of isolated evolution remains, pristine. Near the center of the bog the trail turns right, uphill to the observation platform just as the other end of the Hanalilolilo Trail comes in from the left. Retrace your steps to return.

Island of Oahu

Oahu has over 80 percent of the population of the Hawaiian Islands. As could be expected, few of its trails provide a long wilderness experience such as those on Maui, Hawaii, and Kauai. Nevertheless, many day hikes on Oahu are well worth taking, and can be nicely combined with activities that Honolulu offers. In many cases these trails are accessible by bus for a nominal fare and yet lead through comparatively unpopulated country.

Oahu's longer trails generally cross federal or private land and require extensive efforts to gain access to them. For example, the Waianae Range, the drier of the two mountain ranges on Oahu, could offer good camping and hiking. However, access into it is quite limited. The 3-day Pupukea Ridge Trail following the crest of the Koolau Range has not been included in this book. Permission can be obtained from the Army at Schofield Barracks, but the process is time consuming and cumbersome.

Numerous short and medium length trails accessible to the public lead into the Koolau Range; most are described in this book.

Hibiscus

Camping is difficult because the range is on the wet, windward side of the island and level ground is limited. To compensate, the vegetation is lush and varied. Permits are required from either the Division of Forestry and Wildlife or the Division of State Parks.

The hikes up to the spine of the Koolau Range have a quiet, natural beauty that contrasts with the hectic pace of the Honolulu area. The native Hawaiian forest remains unspoiled high on the range, where rainfall sometimes exceeds 250 inches a year. There are occasional glimpses of the island and the seacoast through breaks in the clouds. The trade winds sweep the heights steadily and with great force. One returns with a broadened perspective for facing the day-to-day problems of civilization.

Other trails follow the lower spur ridges

Windward Oahu from the Pali

Norfolk Island pine grove

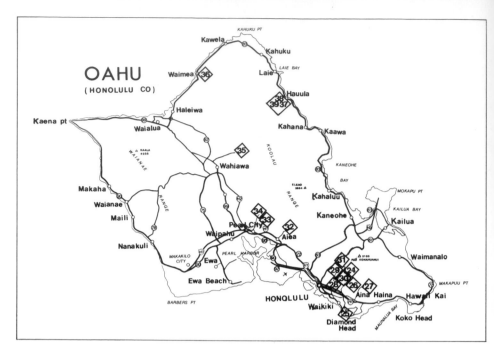

of the Koolau Range and lead partially up its side valleys. These trails do not reach the rain forest, but give a good taste of nature in Hawaii. These lower elevations have a great variety of plant life, both introduced and native. Here, the newly introduced plants are filling the ecological niches once occupied by native species. The region has thriving eucalyptus and Norfolk Island pine forests and a diminishing number of ohia lehua and koa trees. The trails near Hauula on the northeast corner of Oahu lead through such areas.

Two of the trails described on Oahu are in or near heavily populated areas, but they are included because of their diverse and special nature. The Judd Memorial Trail leads through a now thriving and soil-preserving forest of imported species typical of the reforestation efforts of the early 1900's. The trail in Diamond Head Crater offers a view of an impressive volcanic crater and the contemporary ruins of the fortress it became. It is also a reminder of the role Hawaii played during the war in the Pacific.

The Waimea Falls Stream Trail, on the North Coast, is the only trail described in the book that is located in a private park. It has an extraordinary collection of plants, including ones that, alas, are being saved from extinction only in such preserves.

Bracket fungus

Crest of the Koolau Range

Jackass Ginger Pool

24. Manoa Falls

1 hour in, 3/4 hour out
450 calories; difficulty A
0.8 miles one way
Highest point: 1200 feet
Elevation gain: 800 feet
Map: Honolulu 1:24,000
Division of Forestry and Wildlife

The Manoa Falls Trail is the most easily reached of the trails close to Honolulu. The trail is not long, but the dense, rainy forest through which it passes has a great variety of introduced and native plants. Part of the way the trail follows a charming stone footpath through the dense forest. The area's annual rainfall of over 100 inches makes the trail muddy. However, the warm rain at this low elevation should not deter the hiker; the plentiful mosquitoes are less active in the rain. Swimming suits or shorts are probably the best rain gear.

A pool at the base of the falls is big enough for children to wade in. Avoid the pool in high water since rocks may be swept over the falls at these times. Do not climb beyond the falls into the closed watershed. Entry is strictly prohibited by law. Rescue efforts there have led to court appearances and fines. Those with irrepressible energies can make the hard climb to Pauoa Flats up the contouring and zigzagging, but not steep, Aihualoma Trail. Its lower end joins the Manoa Falls Trail shortly before the falls.

Route: Drive up Manoa Road to Paradise Park and Lyon Arboretum near the upper end of Manoa Road in Honolulu's Manoa Valley. Alternatively, take Bus 5, Ala Moana-Manoa, with a Paradise Park sign, to the end of the line at the head of the Manoa Valley. Walk up Manoa Road past Paradise Park and Lyon Arboretum. The road is blocked by a chain barrier fifty yards past Lyon Arboretum, just where a driveway comes up from the wooden houses on the right. The trail starts at the barrier. Go around it and follow the broad dirt path.

The trail leads over a small footbridge across Aihualama Stream and up into the forest reserve. It soon crosses a small stream flowing through a grove of eucalyptus. Beyond the eucalyptus grove, the trail leads along Waihi Stream and passes over the old stone footpath in several places. The trail follows close to the northwest bank of Waihi Stream, but never crosses it. It passes by tangled hau groves, guava, mountain apple, African tulip trees, and ti plants. Toward the end, the trail switchbacks up two small muddy grades before it arrives at the falls.

Manoa Falls Trail

25. Diamond Head (Point Leahi)

¾ hours up, ½ hour down
300 calories; difficulty B
0.7 miles one way
Highest point: 760 feet
Elevation gain: 550 feet
Map: Honolulu 1:24,000
Division of State Parks

Diamond Head, well known from posters and postcards, is not only a landmark but also an elaborate World War I and II fortress, which commanded the artillery defenses of leeward Oahu and its strategic ports. Extensive fortifications and tunnels for the fire control areas of the fort were built into the walls of this late Pleistocene tuff (consolidated volcanic ash) cone. These cleverly concealed fortifications are difficult to see from the ground or air and would be costly to attack from the outside of the crater. They can, however, be easily reached by this short trail from the inside. This can be an enjoyable hike for a family because it is short and there is an air of adventure surrounding the old fortifications. However, children must not be allowed to stray off the trail to steep and dangerous areas.

Route: Drive or take Bus 58 to the intersection of Diamond Head Road and 18th Avenue on the northeast side of Diamond Head Crater. The road into the crater begins just west of the intersection. Follow the road 0.7 miles to the tunnel leading into the crater. The tunnel is closed from 6 pm to 6 am. Drive through the tunnel to the parking area where the trailhead is located.

Walk along the wide, paved walkway toward the crater's southwest wall. The trail, bordered by a handrail, soon leaves the flat and winds up to an overlook giving a view of the interior of the crater. The trail then climbs 78 steps leading to a dark, angular tunnel. A flashlight is helpful here, though light is soon visible and the rail acts as a guide through the tunnel. On its far side a steep flight of 99 steps leads into the lowest level of the fire control station which

Crater wall

once commanded the gun batteries on leeward Oahu. From this level a spiral steel staircase of 43 steps leads up to higher levels. The route then leads out through an opening in the fortification onto the last 53 steps up the observation post atop Point Leahi.

The post, the highest point on the rim, commands a view of all leeward Oahu from Koko Head to Waianae. Rainbows and summer breezes now stand watch.

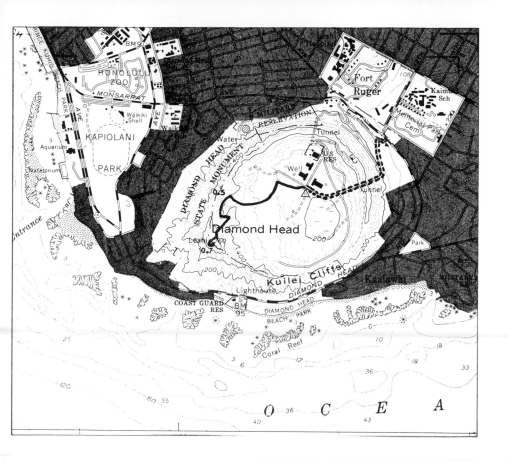

View from Point Leahi

26. Waahila (St. Louis Heights)
2 hours up, 1½ hours down
900 calories; difficulty B
2 miles one way
Highest point: 1700 feet
Elevation gain: 700 feet
Map: Honolulu 1:24,000
Division of Forestry and Wildlife

An extensive native forest and spectacular views make this easily accessible trail in the Honolulu area an exceptionally enjoyable day hike. Despite its proximity to the city, the knife-edged ridge that the trail follows assures you that your only company will be fellow hikers. The trail first passes through groves of Norfolk Island pine, ironwood, and guava. It then leads higher to groves of large native koa and ohia trees with dense undergrowth of ferns and large ti plants. The gullies ending against the main ridge support a wide variety of native trees and shrubs. Except for a few minor boulder scrambles which require caution, the trail is generally easy and well maintained. There is no water along the trail. However, there are fountains, eating pavilions, and restrooms in Waahila Ridge State Park at the trailhead. Those choosing to stop for lunch at one of the viewpoints will be pleased to discover that the wind has blown the mosquitoes away to easier pickings in the valleys below.

Route: Drive to the top of St. Louis Heights and turn down Ruth Place to the Waahila Ridge State Park. Parking is available during daylight hours at the uphill end of the recreation area. Alternatively, take Bus 14, St. Louis Heights, to the end of the line on St. Louis Heights and walk down Ruth Place to the state park entrance. Turn uphill to the right just inside the entrance. Follow the broad path uphill paralleling the fenced boundary of the recreation area through a handsome grove of Norfolk Island pine to the parking area.

Several trails lead from the parking area up the ridge, but all soon come together as the ridge narrows. The main trail is centered

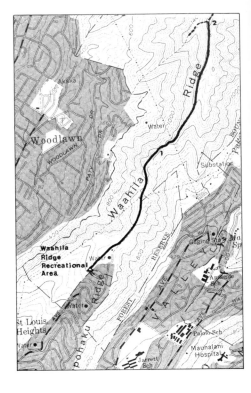

on the ridge and is broad enough for the first 400 yards to serve as a fire road. Some of the paralleling side trails provide intriguing though confusing tours under canopies of guava and ironwood on deep carpets of needles. About 400 yards from the start, the trail splits just before reaching powerlines crossing over the ridge. One fork continues up the ridge to pass between the two sets of poles on the ridge top. The other drops to the left, passing on the sidehill to the far side of the poles. Both trails quickly rejoin. The trail loses 100 feet of elevation, gains a hundred, loses it, and

Ironwood with Koolau Range in background

then progresses generally uphill along the ridge and under one additional powerline.

At 2.0 miles from the start, the trail splits. The main trail turns left and descends steeply from the ridge through a guava forest resounding with the calls of numerous species of imported birds. At the bottom of this descent, the trail hits a gravelled extension of Alani Drive leading to the Woodlawn area in the Manoa Valley. The righthand branch of the trail continues on up the ridge but should not be taken since it leads to a restricted Honolulu watershed.

27. Mauumae (Lanipo)

3 hours up, 2 hours down
1600 calories; difficulty B
3 miles one way
Highest point: 2500 feet
Elevation gain: 1800 feet
Elevation loss: 300 feet
Maps: Honolulu, Koko Head 1:24,000
Division of Forestry and Wildlife

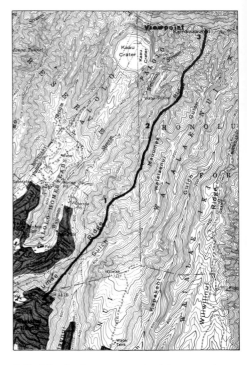

This steep, challenging trail leads up to a 2,500-foot-high view of windward Oahu, Olomana Peak, Maunawili Valley, and Kaneohe from the top of the Koolau Pali. Since much of the trail goes through a fairly dry part of Oahu, it is especially good for reaching the pali (cliffs) during poor weather. The lower part of the trail passes through generally dry forest and grassy patches which provide good views of Honolulu and the surrounding valleys. There are fine places for secluded picnics. Carry water; none is available on this ridgeline trail.

Route: From Waialae Avenue in Kaimuki drive up Wilhelmina Rise and Sierra Drive to Maunalani Circle. Alternatively, take Bus 14 to Maunalani Heights. Go to the highest point on the line, Lurline Drive, and walk to the circle. The trail starts on the Koko Head (east) side of the cyclone-fenced water reservoir area located above Maunalani Circle and passes between two parallel cylcone fences for the first 135 paces. It shortly reaches the spine of the Mauumae Ridge and follows it for the rest of the hike. The ridge dips 200 feet and then climbs steadily all the way to Kainawaanui, a peak on the Koolau Range.

After the initial descent, the trail passes through thickets of staghorn fern, then past large koa trees and ohia lehua. The trail provides one of the few good vantage points of Kaau Crater, an ash and lava cone formed within the last 150,000 years. Kaau Crater is located in closed watershed area No. 1 across Waiomao Stream. Because so few people go into the watershed area, wild pigs may sometimes be seen at a distance on the grass-covered floor of the crater. Nor-folk Island pine, guava, and ironwood are found along the lower portions of the route. Higher up, the trail passes into a native Hawaiian ohia lehua forest. The trail is steep, rough in some places, and can be slippery after rain, but it is easy to follow. In any case, stay on the spine of the Mauumae Ridge, and you will not stray far off the trail.

False staghorn fern, wawaeiole, swordfern

Mauumae Ridge and the Koolau Range

28. Makiki Valley Loop

2-hour loop
600 calories; difficulty A
2-mile loop
Highest point: 1000 feet
Elevation gain: 700 feet
Map: Honolulu 1:24,000
Division of Forestry and Wildlife

The upper Makiki Valley, above Punchbowl, is a lush pocket of tropical forest surrounded by civilization. This forest reserve, the closest to Waikiki and downtown Honolulu, abounds with guava, lilikoi (passion fruit), and mountain apple; yet, only wild pigs and the rare hiker sample their succulent fruits. Numerous species of plants, native and introduced, crowd the area. Small streams sufficient for cooling feet are banked by ginger, taro, and a profusion of flowers. Wild pigs, oblivious to the city a few hundred yards away, quietly roam the forest.

The Makiki Valley Loop is made up of three trails, which form a route up, across, and back down the valley. The Kanealole Trail starts at the Division of Forestry and Wildlife baseyard at the bottom of the valley and leads up to the Makiki Valley Trail, which contours across the valley to join the Maunalaha Trail leading back down to the baseyard.

Route: To reach the Division of Forestry and Wildlife baseyard, go up Makiki Street to Makiki Heights Drive. Follow Makiki Heights Drive about 0.5 miles to the first right turn, where a straight, narrow paved road leads through a state arboretum directly to the baseyard about 400 yards away. The corridor is lined with rows of crimson-flowered African tulip trees and an interesting assortment of other exotic plants, many of which are labeled.

Alternatively, take Bus 15, Pacific Heights, to the intersection of Mott-Smith Drive and Makiki Heights Drive. Walk down Makiki Heights Drive about 0.5 miles to the first left turn, which is the road to the baseyard, and follow it to its end.

Banana plants

Both ends of the loop trail leave from the Division of Forestry and Wildlife baseyard. However, the western trail (the Kanealole Trail) up Kanealole Stream, is the better ascent. This trail is located at the very upper end of the road leading to the baseyard. It follows the course of an abandoned road and is somewhat muddy. About 0.7 miles from its beginning the trail joins the Makiki Valley Trail proceeding across the valley. At this junction the Makiki Valley Trail contours left to Tantalus Drive and right to Round Top Drive. Follow the Makiki Valley Trail right, across the valley, cross-

Makiki Trail

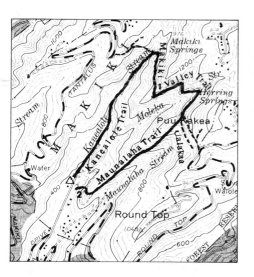

The descent follows a ridgeline for the most part, passing through kukui, eucalyptus, sandalwood, and juniper. The trail passes by interesting rock formations and provides good views of Honolulu. This trail is fairly dry and the switchbacks make the final downhill to the baseyard easy going. The trail crosses a footbridge at the baseyard.

ing Kanealole and Moleka Streams. About 200 paces after the Moleka Stream crossing several trails intersect. The Maunalaha Trail goes down to the right to the baseyard. The Ualakaa Trail leads straight ahead; the Makiki Trail turns left and then contours right to Round Top Drive. To make the loop trip, descend to the baseyard by the Maunalaha Trail.

29. Manoa Cliffs

2 hours in, 2 hours out
800 calories; difficulty B
3 miles one way
Highest point: 1900 feet
Elevation gain: 500 feet
Map: Honolulu 1:24,000
Division of Forestry and Wildlife

A wide variety of plant life with many species tagged for identification and a thrilling section skirting along the forested cliffs above the Manoa Valley recommend this day hike. Included among the tagged plants are native white hibiscus, kopiko, ohia lehua, kalia, tree fern, mountain apple, mountain naupaka, and koa. These and other species make this trail a favorite field trip for botany students from the nearby University of Hawaii. The trail leads first through ginger, guava, and banana and then onto the cliffs above the Manoa Valley, offering views of the area above Manoa Falls and the whole Manoa Valley. Use caution on the precipitous parts of the trail since the cliffs covered with vegetation are deceptively steep.

Route: Beginning near the northwest (mountain) side of Punchbowl, drive up Tantalus Drive almost to its top, where Tantalus Drive begins to contour right and a concrete driveway leads straight ahead uphill to the Hawaiian Telephone Company facilities. The trail begins just to the left of this driveway. The trail contours along the northwest side of Tantalus past several small streambeds. About one mile from its start, the trail turns sharply to the right, almost reversing itself, and switchbacks up the hill above Pauoa Flats. Just at this turn, a trail from Pauoa Flats leads in from straight ahead. Care must be exercised to avoid following the trail leading to Pauoa Flats since it may appear to be the main trail. The switchbacks on the Manoa Cliffs Trail lead up through encroaching ginger. Soon the Puu Ohia Trail comes steeply up from Pauoa Flats on the left to join the Manoa Cliffs Trail and leaves again uphill

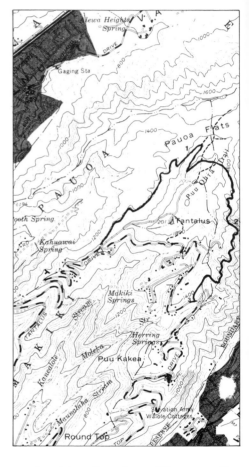

to the right after about 200 paces. The Manoa Cliffs Trail continues on to contour along the spectacular cliffs above the Manoa Valley. Finally, almost three miles from its start, the trail leads up, right, over a low ridge, and then down to Round Top Drive. You can follow Round Top Drive right, back to the trailhead 1.5 miles away, or return the way you came.

Bamboo grove

30. Puu Ohia (Tantalus)

2 hours up, 1¾ hours down
800 calories; difficulty B
2 miles one way
Highest point: 2000 feet
Elevation gain: 500 feet
Elevation loss: 400 feet
Map: Honolulu 1:24,000
Division of Forestry and Wildlife

This day hike goes over the top of Puu Ohia (Tantalus), a lush, forested hill with thick bamboo, Norfolk Island pine, and eucalyptus. It eventually leads to a view of the Nuuanu Valley and windward Oahu. A short side trail leads to the small Puu Ohia (Tantalus) Crater. The wide variety of plants, the expansive view at its end, and its proximity to Honolulu and the University of Hawaii make this one of the most heavily traveled trails on Oahu.

Route: The trailhead is located opposite a parking area fifty yards west of the highest point on Round Top and Tantalus Drives. Initially the trail switchbacks uphill through guava, ferns, and thickets of bamboo. About 0.5 miles from the start it passes short side trails, one of which leads right, down into Puu Ohia (Tantalus) Crater. Proceed on the main trail, which soon reaches a concrete service road leading up from Tantalus Drive. Follow the road to the right, toward the mountains and to the telephone buildings at the end. The trail continues toward the mountains from directly behind the telephone buildings and heads downhill along a path cut through a thick grove of bamboo. The path soon angles right to join the Manoa Cliffs Trail.

At this junction turn left to follow the Manoa Cliffs Trail for about 200 paces to where the trail to Pauoa Flats leads steeply downhill to a paperbark grove. A confusing array of trails in the grove seems to lead left and right. To get to the lookout above the Nuuanu Valley, continue straight ahead on the well-used trail across the flats, over a maze of exposed and muddy tree roots. The trail veers slightly to the right as it leaves the flats.

It reaches the lookout 0.7 miles after leaving muddy Pauoa Flats, passing the Aihualama Trail on the way. Thick forest of paperbark, bamboo, eucalyptus, and banyan trees darkens the route. Mosquitoes are aggressive, and rain and mud are plentiful. Do not go beyond the lookout into the closed watershed area.

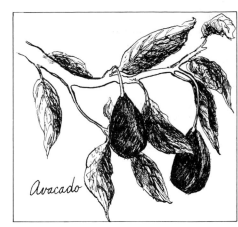

Avacado

Climbing screwpine (ieie)

Nuuanu Valley

31. Judd Memorial
(Jackass Ginger Pool)

1-hour loop
250 calories; difficulty A
1.3-mile loop
Highest point: 700 feet
Elevation gain: 300 feet
Map: Honolulu 1:24,000
Division of Forestry and Wildlife

This short trail is ideal for families. In a few places the route is difficult to determine. However, the trail is short, well graded, and passes through pleasant groves of eucalyptus, Norfolk Island pine, and hau trees. Steep, dangerously slippery side trails lead off the main trail.

The trail is named after Charles S. Judd, Territorial Forester from 1914-1939. Judd was one of the foresters of the early 1900's through whose dedication and planning large areas of the Hawaiian Islands were reforested after the thorough and prodigal destruction of the rare native forests by imported livestock. They planted many varieties of imported trees, most noticeably Norfolk Island pine and various species of eucalyptus. The trail passes through an area typical of such a soil-saving reforestation effort. Apart from the hau trees close to the stream course, virtually all the species of vegetation to be seen along the trail are new to Hawaii.

Route: Take Bus 4, Nuuanu-Dowsett, up Nuuanu Pali Drive to its stop just before Kimo Drive, shortly before the end of the line. Walk up Nuuanu Pali Drive about 0.7 miles to the downhill side of the short bridge over the Reservoir Two spillway. By car, go up Nuuanu Pali Drive to the Reservoir Two spillway about 0.7 miles past Kimo Drive and just past Poli Hiwa Place. At this point the trail begins, leading directly downhill and east at a right angle to the road. the trail reaches Nuuanu Stream within 50 yards. Rock-hop across the stream and proceed up the far side through a thicket of bamboo, side-hilling up into a grove of turpentine trees. Thereafter the trail rounds a small ridge through a

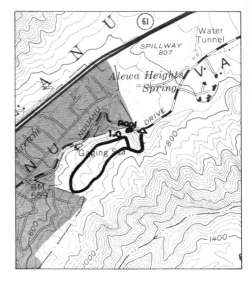

eucalyptus grove free of underbrush. It then leads into a grove of Norfolk Island pine. The trail has been all but obliterated where it rounds the small ridge, but the trail leading into the Norfolk Island pine grove is well maintained. It contours easily through the Norfolk Island pine to the boundary of the forest reserve where it approaches a residential area near Ragsdale Place. Several confusing side trails lead sharply up or down from the main trail.

At the residential area the trail switchbacks downhill and then begins to return upstream under tangles of hau trees and guava. Within a few minutes walk from the residential area, the trail reaches a bank about 75 feet above Nuuanu Stream. Follow along the bank. Within 3 or 4 minutes after contouring up through a couple of small gullies, the trail forks. One fork leads down a scramble to the swimming

Jackass Ginger Pool

hole, Jackass Ginger Pool (Kahuailanawai). The other fork leads by several routes up the ridge to the trail back.

A clearly apparent alternative trail returns up the far side of Nuuanu Stream from the swimming hole to the highway. Mosquitoes are usually numerous near the swimming hole, especially in shaded areas.

32. Aiea Loop

3-hour loop
800 calories; difficulty A
4.8-mile loop
Highest point: 1600 feet
Elevation gain: 700 feet
Elevation loss: 200 feet
Maps: Kaneohe, Waipahu 1:24,000
Division of State Parks

This well-maintained, graded trail passes through a handsome forest. It is a favorite for whole families, from grandparents to small children. About 60 years ago, the area was reforested with Norfolk Island pine, ironwood, brush box, albizzia, and several varieties of eucalyptus. The upper portion of the trail has a covering of native trees and shrubs including ohia lehua, koa, and some sandalwood. In the lower portion the introduced species have replaced the unique Hawaiian species. Since it is located in Keaiwa Heiau State Recreation Area, you can combine the hike with picnics at the park's pavilions or roadside camping (by permit).

The foundation of a *heiau* (temple), formerly used by *kahuna* (Hawaiian priests) practicing medicine, is located at the park and is still in good condition. Labeled examples of medicinal plants used by the kahuna are located near the heiau. At the time of Captain Cook (1778) the kahuna who used such plants were at least as successful in the art of healing as their European counterparts, according to Richard McBride in his book, *Kahuna.* The kahuna had specialists for particular fields of medicine. The heiau at the park was used by the *kahuna la'au lapa'au,* the pharmacologists and general practitioners of the time.

Along the eastern part of the loop is the wreckage of a C-47 cargo plane which crashed in 1943. Parts of the plane are still visible through the dense foliage. The park gates are open only during daylight hours.

Route: Start at Aiea Heights Drive in Aiea. Follow it to its end at the park. If traveling by Bus 11, Aiea Heights, get off

Campground

where Kaamilo Road rejoins Aiea Heights and walk about 1.5 miles up Aiea Heights Drive to the well-marked park entrance. The trail starts at the extreme upper end of the main road in the park and leads along the ridgeline, continuing up the ridge steadily until it returns via the ridge to the east. On the trip out, stay on the main trail since several secondary trails lead in and out. The trip along the east ridge gives good views of the Koolau Range to the north and of the surrounding forest.

About two-thirds of the way down the east ridge, the trail passes the wreckage of the C-47, half-buried in a small gully on the right below the trail. Apparently the plane

Aiea Loop Trail

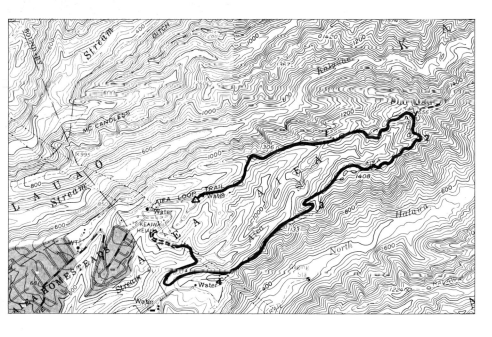

crashed higher on the ridge and over time the wreckage has tumbled down into the small gully. Shortly past the wreck, a side trail, originating at Camp Smith, comes in from the left. The main trail then descends to Aiea Stream, passing through guava and hau trees. It passes under powerlines twice, once on the descent to the stream and again as the trail intersects the stream. The trail then climbs steadily for a short distance along a small gully, past a hau thicket and then into the park camping area next to the road.

33. Waimano

5 hours up, 4½ hours down
1750 calories; difficulty C
7 miles one way
Highest point: 2200 feet
Elevation gain: 1600 feet
Maps: Oahu 1:62,500
      Kaneohe, Waipahu 1:24,000
Division of Forestry and Wildlife

This long trail takes you through some of the most lovely country on Oahu, passing a small swimming hole on the way and leading to a spectacular view of windward Oahu from high on the Koolau Pali. The trail provides many good vantage points as it climbs along the cliffsides above Waimano Stream. Unless overgrown beyond the swimming hole, it is possible to follow the trail all the way to the crest of the Koolau Range.

Route: Take H-1 from Honolulu towards Pearl City and turn off at the Waimalu exit to Pearl City. Join Moanalua Road and after a mile turn right onto Waimano Home Road. Follow Waimano Home Road towards the mountains for 2.2 miles to its end at the Waimano Home security fence and guard house. Alternatively, take the Pacific Palisades Bus, to where it leaves Waimano Home Road (Koko Mai Drive) to go to Pacific Palisades. From there walk or take the infrequent Shuttle Bus 71 up Waimano Home Road a mile to the guard house.

The trail begins across from the guardhouse and just before the fence. It splits immediately into an upper and a lower route. Take the upper route, following the fence and the course of an abandoned irrigation ditch and tunnels. The lower, better-maintained route, preferable for the return, follows an old jeep road down to Waimano Stream and eventually climbs steeply to combine with the upper trail about a mile from the trailhead.

Beyond this junction the trail follows the ditch until the ditch ends at a small stream and the remnants of a small diversion dam about 2.5 miles from the trailhead. Cross the stream and turn right. Within a few yards, the trail passes an abandoned irriga-

Windward Oahu from the Pali

tion tunnel through the ridge on the left (north) side of the stream. It soon switchbacks up a short distance to the crest of the ridge.

The trail then follows a cliff edge above Waimano Stream. About 3.3 miles from its start, the trail reaches a dam and pool near the confluence of Waimano Stream and a tributary from the south. At this point the trail crosses Waimano Stream on a small dam and then follows the stream bed up about 30 yards to the confluence of the two streams. It then crosses the left (north) branch and proceeds upstream to follow a course on the ridge between the two branches to the crest of the Koolau Range. The trail beyond is poorly maintained and heavy brush encroaches. Only well-conditioned and experienced hikers should proceed beyond this point. With long pants and sleeves and ample time, the trip is worth taking. This portion of the trail leads through magnificent scenery to a spectacular, windswept viewpoint of windward Oahu from the top of the high Koolau Pali.

The first dam

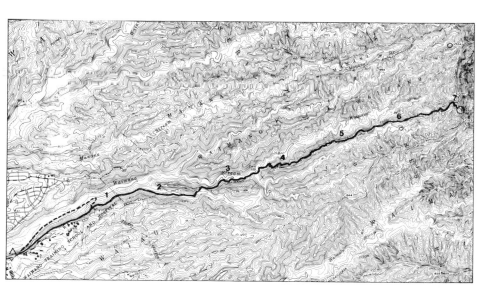

34. Manana

5 hours up, 4 hours down
1800 calories; difficulty C
7 miles one way
Highest point: 2660 feet
Elevation gain: 1700 feet
Maps: Oahu 1:62,500
          Kaneohe, Waipahu 1:24,000
Division of Forestry and Wildlife

If you have felt the need to escape from the pressures of population and civilization on Oahu, this is the trail for you. Little used, rough, and not by any stretch of the imagination improved, it leads into one of the truly wild areas on Oahu. Mud is always plentiful, and in many places brush encroaches on the trail, so suitable clothing must be worn. Hikers should dress for rain since the upper reaches of the trail are in an area that receives up to 200 inches of rain per year. Despite all this, the view and the wilderness at the end of thc trail are worth the effort.

Route: Drive to Waimano Home Road near Pearl City. Proceed on Waimano Home Road about 1.2 miles, then left onto Komo Mai Drive. Follow Komo Mai Drive to the top of Pacific Palisades. Alternatively, take Bus 53, Pacific Palisades, to the top of Pacific Palisades and walk about three blocks to the end of Komo Mai Drive. From the end of Komo Mai Drive, pass through the Board of Water Supply gate on foot and follow the paved road to the trailhead in the forest reserve, passing under powerlines and by a water tank.

The trail follows the ridgeline all the way to the Koolau Range. It first passes through an extensive burned area with regenerating eucalyptus trees and a heavy undergrowth of false staghorn fern. At times the trail may be steep and difficult to follow, but keep to the ridgeline and you will rejoin it. The trail may be confusing as the ridgeline nears the spine of the Koolau Range. Note the route carefully for the return trip. Being lost in this area would be a serious matter.

If the weather breaks, the top provides outstanding views of windward Oahu and

White Ginger Blossom

Kaneohe Bay. The vegetation is typical of the native rain forest. A dense underbrush of ferns, mosses, and shrubs makes for extremely rough going if you leave the trail. The winds over the Pali are exceptionally strong in this area. Because of the length of the trail and the roughness of the country, carry a flashlight, food, a map, and a compass. Keep track of the amount of daylight you have left. The sun goes down quickly at these latitudes. At the top of the Koolau Pali a difficult and dangerous route leads southeast (right) over to the Waimano Trail, a mile distant, following the ridgeline and passing an old plane wreck. This trip should not be attempted without adequate time, planning, and an experienced party.

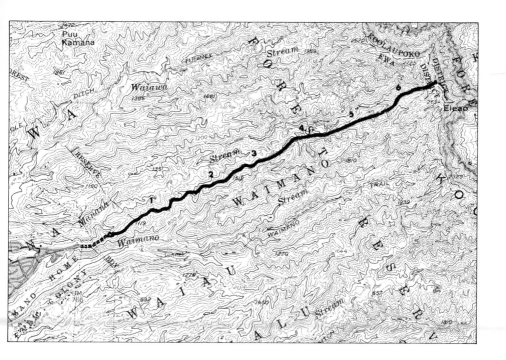

Manana Trail through Regenerating Eucalyptus

35. Poamoho Ridge

2½ hours up, 2 hours down
1200 calories; difficulty B
3.4 miles one way
Highest point: 2500 feet
Elevation gain: 600 feet
Maps: Oahu 1:62,500
       Hauula 1:24,000
Division of Forestry and Wildlife

The Poamoho Ridge Trail provides relatively easy access to the top of the Koolau Range and one of the best vantage points on the Island of Oahu. There is an exceptionally good view of the Pali and the shore of windward Oahu from the windswept, green meadow at the end of the trail. The trail leads through some of the wildest area in Oahu — rain forests with no human inhabitants. It passes close to one of the two Division of Forestry and Wildlife cabins now located on the Koolau Range. These simple cabins have no furniture but provide shelter from the frequent rains at this elevation. Contact the Division of Forestry and Wildlife in Honolulu in advance to use the cabins.

Route: Access to the trail is across private land, and prior permission to pass must be obtained. Contact the Division of Forestry and Wildlife in Honolulu for current information about obtaining access. To reach the trailhead, drive on the Kamehameha Highway from Honolulu to the Dole pineapple stand past the town of Wahiawa. Take the first turnoff to right just after the pineapple stand. Drive, through the fields, towards Helemano radio station and turn right onto the loop road around it. At the far side of the loop, follow the dirt road through the fields east toward the Koolau Range until you reach the forest reserve boundary. From the boundary drive 2.4 miles up the road into the forest reserve. Keep to the ridge top. Continue on past a road from the right leading out of the nearby streambed. The ridgetop road is quite rough. If it becomes too rough for your vehicle, proceed on foot.

The road eventually turns into a trail. Parking is available at this point. Follow this obvious trail steadily upward. A small stream with clear water crosses the trail at about two miles. A little after three miles the trail reaches the summit of the Koolau Range and intersects the Koolau Summit Trail, which follows the Koolau ridgetop to the left and right of the intersection.

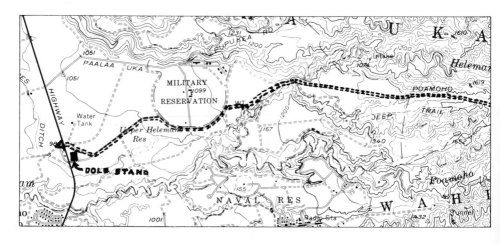

Poamoho Cabin, maintained by the Division of Forestry and Wildlife, is located to the right (south) about half an hour along the Koolau Summit Trail. It is prudent to take a plastic ground cover since the area is usually wet, but has many beautiful places for picnics. Even if the area is cloud covered, as it usually is, there are often short breaks in the clouds which offer chances for some of the most spectacular photographs in Hawaii.

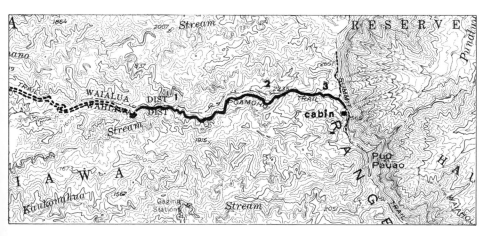

36. Waimea Falls Stream

2-hour loop
300 calories; difficulty A
1.8-mile loop
Highest point: 200 feet
Elevation gain: 200 feet
Map: Waimea 1:24,000
Waimea Falls Park; private,
admission charge

Nowhere is the extinction of species more evident than in the Hawaiian Islands. For millions of years this island chain, rising from the ocean floor and separated by vast distances from other lands, was a world onto itself. Life forms from the outside established themselves only at rare intervals. These had much scope to evolve, free of competition, into varied new species, eventually occupying the islands' empty ecological niches.

The Polynesians first sailed into this isolation a millennia and a half ago bringing taro, ti, banana, pigs, rats, flies, and many other new plants and animals to the islands. The aggressive new life forms which the Hawaiians introduced and their own activities began the destruction of the unique and vulnerable species inhabiting the islands.

For a time, the great distances worked to again isolate the islands from the outside. Eventually, a tall-masted ship of discovery gave knowledge of these islands to all the world. There followed, for good and ill, the arrival of many races of people and common plants and animals of all sorts: cattle, goats, mosquitoes, thorns, and thistles. What once existed was crowded out, tilled, eaten, and burned until little remains, except in remote areas.

A Kokia cookei tree grows in the gardens of Waimea Falls Park. It was the last of its species until cuttings from it were planted in other gardens. Its hibiscus-like flowers are a lovely, deep red. Nearby is a collection of endangered Hawaiian flora, one of the largest in the world. Here one may gain an impression of primordial Hawaii. Sadly, outside such protection these plants move rapidly toward extinction. Besides this fine

Along the trail

collection, the gardens contain extensive collections of plants used by the Hawaiians and rare plants imported from islands all over the world.

Route: Waimea Falls Park is about five miles northeast of Haleiwa, off Highway 83, which circles windward Oahu. A marked turn-off leads inland from the highway at Waimea Bay, up Waimea Stream, half a mile to the park entrance. Circle Island Bus 52 goes past the turn-off leading to the park. There is a reasonable charge for admission to the park.

To reach the Waimea Falls Stream Trail take the main walkway inside the park. Walk past the tram terminal. The trailhead is on the left, just before reaching the bridge

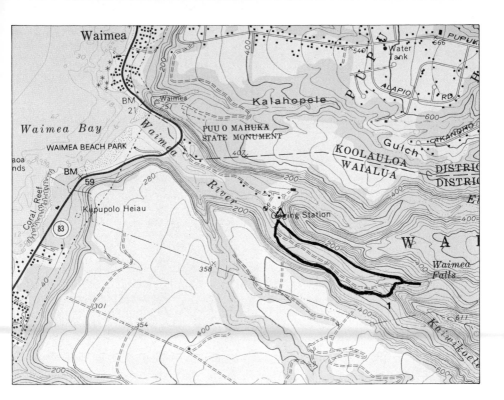

over Waimea Stream. Follow the wide gravel path with the stream on the right and a lilicaea collection on the left, soon passing through a tall canopy of bamboo. The trail then narrows, staying close to the stream, and eventually reaches a fork with two branches up the stream, one near it and one above it. The branches rejoin in about 150 yards. At 0.7 miles the trail reaches the tram turn-around. Continue ahead to plunging Waimea Falls and the various tourist facilities. You may wish to stop for a pleasant swim in the pool at the base of the falls.

Start your return along the tram route, but soon after crossing the stream turn left and up steps at a sign marked "hiking trail." The trail leads through several botanical collections, a hula and games area and eventually reaches a wedding stage, a Hawaiian living site and other Hawaiian stonework. Since the trail parallels the garden area, it is possible to drop down to see areas of interest and return to the trail. Allow ample time to see the specimens.

Waimea Falls Park has many other trails, with access by special permission. The park arranges hikes for groups in its 1,800 acres

Waimea Falls

of wilderness area. More information can be obtained from Waimea Falls Park, 59-864 Kamehameha Hwy, Haleiwa, HI 96712, tel. (808) 638-8511.

37. Maakua Ridge

2-hour loop
600 calories; difficulty A
2.5 mile loop
Highest Point: 650 feet
Elevation gain: 800 feet
Map: Hauula 1:24,000

The Maakua Ridge Trail is a pleasant, easy hike traversing a botanical battleground. Legions of the aggressive new arrival, Costa's Curse *(Climedia hirta)*, are invading and driving out the plants of the older Hawaiian landscape. In the lower regions Christmas Berry has already won the battle and holds the ground so thickly that tunnels through the brush have been cut for the trail. Hala, ti plants, and ferns typical of Hawaiian landscape before the arrival of the Europeans are still prevalent along the upper portions of the trail.

In the early morning the webs of enterprising spiders lace the trail. The spiders drop quickly to the ground in fright at your approach, except those of a peculiar red and white, crab-like species. Trusting to their armor, these harmless little creatures placidly allow you to approach and photograph them. Their webs, covered with morning dew and always moving in the trade winds, are a beautiful sight.

Route: Drive or take the Circle Island Bus 55 along the Kamehameha Highway (83) to Hauula Beach Park in Hauula. Turn toward the mountains on Hauula Homestead Road, the first road north of Hauula Beach Park. After 0.2 miles, you will reach Maakua Road, just as Hauula Homestead Road veers left. Park by Hauula Homestead Road and walk along Maakua Road about 200 yards until it turns uphill to the right. There the wide, grassy trail leads left, towards the mountains.

In about 125 yards the trail crosses a dry stream bed. About 75 yards after the stream bed the trail comes to a fork. The left fork is the Maakua Gulch Trail, the right fork is the Hauula Loop Trail. Take the left fork to

Trail Tunneling through Christmas Berry

reach the turnoff onto the Maakua Ridge Trail, which starts 150 yards from the junction. The trail immediately crosses the dry bed of Maakua Stream and then switchbacks up the hillside. Part way up, the trail passes the junction with the return leg of the loop, coming in from the left. Continue on, sidehilling toward the mountains, gradually gaining elevation. Ti plants and hala trees come into view.

The trail reaches a ridgeback and climbs fairly steeply for about 200 yards, then drops down into Papali Gulch, located on the southeast side of the main ridge. It

Maakua Gulch

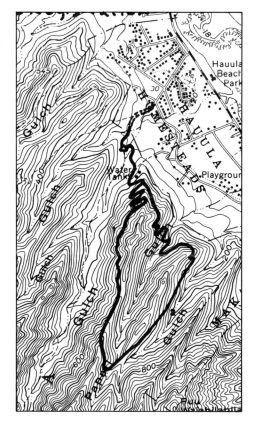

crosses Papali Stream to gain the crest of the next ridge and switchbacks along its southeast side. A broad view of the coast and the sound of the ocean greet you as the trail rounds the base of the ridge to re-enter Papali Gulch in deep thickets of Christmas Berry. The trail switchbacks out of Papali Gulch and rounds the next ridge to complete the loop.

38. Hauula Loop

2-hour loop
500 calories; difficulty A
2.5-mile loop
Highest point: 650 feet
Elevation gain: 600 feet
Map: Hauula 1:24,000
Division of Forestry and Wildlife

The Hauula Loop Trail is one of the three trails on state land near Hauula in windward Oahu. The other two are the Maakua Ridge and Maakua Gulch Trails. The Hauula Trail is the easiest of these trails, since it is well maintained and fairly level. The hike, a gentle loop for the most part, provides good views of the ocean and the nearby settlement of Hauula, passing through groves of planted Norfolk Island pine. Wildflowers and mushrooms grow through the matted needles. The trade winds sweeping over this area have not yet hit the steep, rain-making Pali of the Koolau Range. Thus, the area basks in sun, neighboring the almost perpetual clouds not far inland.

Route: Drive or take Circle Island Bus 55 along Highway 83 to Hauula Beach Park in Hauula. Turn toward the mountains on Hauula Homestead Road, which is the first road north of Hauula Beach Park. After 0.2 miles, Hauula Homestead Road reaches Maakua Road, just as Hauula Homestead Road veers left. Park by Hauula Homestead Road and walk along Maakua Road about 200 yards until it turns uphill to the right. There the wide, grassy trail leads left, towards the mountains. In about 125 yards the trail crosses a usually dry stream bed.

The trail comes to a fork about 75 yards after the stream bed. The left fork leads to the Maakua Gulch Trail and further on, to the Maakua Ridge Trail. The right fork is the correct one for the Hauula Loop Trail. About 90 paces from the fork, the Hauula Loop Trail again crosses the usually dry stream bed. It then proceeds on up the side of the ridge, climbing fairly steeply for the first 300 paces. About halfway up the side of the ridge the return portion of the loop

comes in from the left (west) to join the trail. Go to the right, switchbacking up the side of the ridge. The trail then contours gently around the ridge, crosses Waipilopilo Gulch, and attains the crest of a second, small ridge. It follows the spine of this second ridge up to a good viewpoint of the upland rain forest at the trail's highest point. The loop trail then descends to recross Waipilopilo Gulch, contours to the crest of the first ridge, and angles down its far side to complete the loop and rejoin the main trail. A scattered few examples of native species of plants are found in Waipilopilo Gulch.

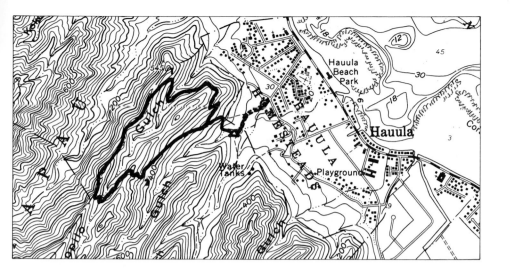

Foothills of Koolau Range

39. Maakua Gulch

3 hours up, 3 hours back
1500 calories; difficulty B
3 miles one way
Highest point: 1200 feet
Elevation gain: 1150 feet
Map: Hauula 1:24,000
Division of Forestry and Wildlife

A dip in a small pool of clear, cool, mountain water at the base of a waterfall is your reward for reaching the end of this somewhat difficult trail. The trail is unimproved for the most part. It is nonexistent for much of its distance, where it follows the bed of Maakua Stream over smooth, slippery, water-worn boulders. When dry, these boulders may provide challenging rock-hopping; however, if they are damp, utmost caution is required to avoid breaks and bruises. The last part of the trail is exceptionally beautiful, passing through kukui groves, stands of mountain apple with their tasty red fruit, and the lush vegetation on the floor of the ever-narrowing canyon. The walls of the canyon narrow until they are but a few feet across, making a deadly trap if there are heavy rains in the mountains upstream or if rocks fall from above.

Route: Drive or take Circle Island Bus 55 along Highway 83 to Hauula Beach Park in Hauula. Turn toward the mountains on Hauula Homestead Road, which is the first road to the north of Hauula Beach Park. Proceed on Hauula Homestead Road for 0.2 miles. At that point, just as Hauula Homestead veers left, you will reach Maakua Road. Park by Hauula Homestead Road. Walk along Maakua Road about 200 yards until it veers uphill, right. There the wide, grassy trail leads left, towards the mountains.

In about 125 yards the trail crosses a dry stream bed and soon comes to a fork. The right fork is the Hauula Loop Trail; the left is the Maakua Gulch Trail. Proceed on the left fork up the valley floor, passing by the Maakua Ridge Trail about 150 paces after the junction with the Hauula Loop Trail.

Falls — Maakua Stream

The Maakua Gulch Trail parallels the usually dry bed of Maakua Stream and soon crosses a small stream coming down from the right. It then continues into the steadily narrowing gulch, crisscrossing the stream bed. The trail ceases to be improved at this point and is strenuous going. However, it is hard to go far wrong since the gulch is narrow and affords no turnoffs. About a mile into the gulch, the trail begins to follow the stream bed itself or, more accurately, the stream bed is the trail. Proceed to the pool and waterfall at the end of the gulch. The pool is deep enough for a few swimming strokes. Beyond it the route becomes too precipitous for further travel.

Forest floor — mushrooms and kukui nuts

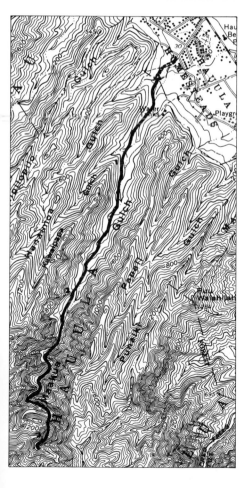

Island of Kauai

Kauai, the early home of Pele, the goddess of volcanism, is the oldest, roughest, and greenest of the Hawaiian Islands. Ever since Pele with her flows of molten lava and showers of volcanic ash left Kauai, erosion has been steadily nibbling at the island with wind, wave, and water. This perseverance has produced a land of rare variety and beauty. The towering, fluted cliffs, waterfalls, and hidden valleys of the Na Pali Coast, the deep Waimea Canyon, and the flat, high, and muddy Alakai Swamp are the masterworks of erosion's craft.

Into these areas lead the trails described in this section. All are located within a very few miles of each other on the northwest corner of Kauai. However, the country is so rugged that each trail leads into a unique area, each with sights quite distinct from the others. One group of trails centers in Waimea Canyon, another around Kokee State Park, and another on the Na Pali Coast. Because of the island's ruggedness, it is necessary to drive nearly all the way around it to reach the Na Pali Coast from the other two groups.

Waimea Canyon, "The Grand Canyon of the Pacific," provides not only spectacular views from its rim, but also wilderness hiking and camping along the streams on the canyon floor. The Kukui Trail leads down the long descent from the rim to Wiliwili Camp near the Waimea River. From Wiliwili Camp, the Koaie Canyon Trail leads up Koaie Stream through the ruins of ancient villages. The difficult journey back up to the canyon rim assures you that there will be few to disturb your solitude on the canyon floor.

Sugi Grove Campground and the camp-ground and cabins at Kokee State Park make good bases of operations for the day hiking trails nearby. These trails lead deep into the remote Alakai Swamp and to splendid vantage points of Waimea Canyon and the Na Pali Coast. The lush beauty of the region bears a small price: it is generally quite wet, and rain must be expected. More trails lead through this area than are described here. A week could easily be spent hiking them.

The Na Pali Coast group centers around the Kalalau Trail. This is the only route along the rugged Na Pali Coast — and even this ends at seacliffs halfway down the coast. From the Kalalau Trail two short trails lead to the falls and pools in lovely side valleys. Several good campsites along the Kalalau Trail are described in the text. Though the area has fewer trails than the Kokee area, the decidedly better weather encourages hikers to dally on the warm, sandy beaches and to view the spectacular headlands.

Kalalau Valley

Hanakapiai Falls

Na Pali Coast

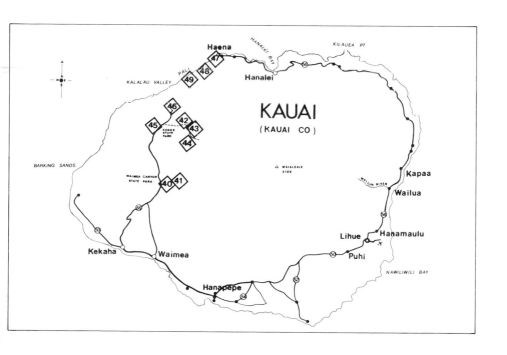

40. Kukui

1¾ hours down, 3 hours up
1600 calories; difficulty B
2.5 miles one way
Highest point: 3000 feet
Elevation loss: 2300 feet
Map: Waimea Canyon 1:24,000
Division of Forestry and Wildlife

LONG & DIFFICULT HIKE TO CANYON FLOOR. EASIER TAKE ILLIAU NATURE LOOP AND WALK DOWN KUKUI TRAIL .5 MILE OR 1 MILE MAX. (NOT A FLAT TRAIL HIKING BOOTS RECOMMENDED)

This steep trail leads into a strange and remote region of Kauai. It can be hiked in one day. However, because of the effort involved and the beauty of the canyon floor, an overnight trip, especially with a side trip to Koaie Canyon (described later) is preferable. The Kukui Trail provides direct public access to the Waimea Canyon floor and its trail network. The climatic change from the usually overcast and somewhat cool and wet top to the warm and dry valley floor 2,300 feet below is pronounced. The return trip is best made in the early morning when the sun's rays are cooler, since even at that time it is an outstanding demon purge.

Route: Take Highway 50 west from Lihue almost all the way through Waimea to Waimea Canyon Drive, beginning on the right at the Waimea Baptist Church. Follow Waimea Canyon Drive for almost 7 miles to Highway 55. Turn uphill to the right onto Highway 55 going toward Kokee State Park. The trailhead is a little over two miles from this junction and 6.8 miles from Kokee Park Headquarters.

Park along the roadside across from the trailhead. Take the Illiau Nature Loop to the wooden sign-in stand close to the canyon's rim. As of this writing, short-term camping for up to three nights is automatically approved upon signing in at the stand at the trailhead. Beyond the sign-in stand the trail switchbacks steeply down the ridge toward the Waimea River over two thousand feet below.

The trail keeps close to the main ridgeline until it reaches a saddle where the ridge rises out to a small promontory. At this point the trail turns left (north) to go down a broad, eroded hillside. Near the bottom of

View across Waimea Canyon

the eroded area, the trail turns right, into the forest, and begins a switchbacking descent down to Wiliwili Camp, the trail's terminus. The camp is located close to the river at the junction of the Waimea River Trail and the Kukui Trail. All along the way forest division white quarter mile markers give some indication of the trail's location.

The Waimea River and the Waimea Canyon Trail, which parallels the river, act as baselines at the bottom of the canyon in case you become lost. Water is unavailable along the trail. The Waimea River and its

Waimea Canyon from Kukui Trail

side streams provide ample water, which, however, should be treated before drinking. A large swimming hole in the river is located a short distance downstream from Wiliwili Camp.

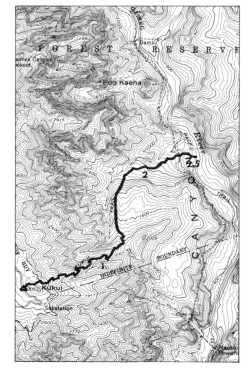

41. Koaie Canyon
   via 40. Kukui
3¼ hours down, 5 hours up
2600 calories; difficulty B
5.5 miles one way
Highest point: 2300 feet
Elevation loss: 2300
Elevation gain: 800 feet
Map: Waimea Canyon 1:24,000
Division of Forestry and Wildlife

Surrounded by high, steep canyon walls and paralleling the course of a large, boulder-filled mountain stream, this trail gives the illusion of being in some alpine region far removed from the Hawaiian Islands. This is all the more peculiar since the trail's elevation scarcely exceeds a thousand feet above sea level. When the trail passes by the terraced ruins of ancient Hawaiian settlements and their extensive stone walls, the illusion is complete. The Andes and Inca ruins come to mind. In actuality this area was populated by upland people who traded the goods of the mountains for those of the sea. It was in woods such as those surrounding this trail that koa trees were grown for the war canoes of the Hawaiians. Although easy to hike, the trail is difficult to reach; thus, few will disturb your musings as you ponder these scenes. For those less given to philosophy, the lovely stream offers excellent swimming holes and smooth rocks for basking in the sun.

Route: The Kukui Trail, described previously, is the only trail providing direct public access to the Koaie Canyon Trail. Starting at Wiliwili Camp, the end of the Kukui Trail, proceed up the Waimea Canyon Trail about 0.4 miles to a river crossing before reaching Poo Kaeha, a promontory on the west side of the Waimea River. Cross the river to the east bank. During stormy weather in the mountains, flash floods and high water make crossings dangerous. If blocked by high water, wait till the water drops before crossing, usually a matter of a few hours.

The Koaie Canyon Trail proceeds a short way up the east bank of the Waimea River, passes a small hunters' shelter, Kaluahaulu

View from Koaie Canyon

Camp, and then leaves the Waimea River to follow the southeast bank of Koaie Stream. The crossing of Hipalau Stream, a small tributary of Koaie Stream, may cause some confusion since the trail may be washed away at this point. If so, follow the fairly level stream course upstream 50 to 100 yards until you reach a small cascade. From here proceed on to the far (east) side of Hipalau Stream to regain the trail. The trail passes numerous stone ruins beginning about a mile from the Waimea River. From the ruins after Hipalau Stream, the trail goes on through occasional dense thickets of kukui trees and guava. The trail ends at Lonomea Camp, a forest reserve open shelter. A swimming hole and perches for leisurely sunbathing are located in the stream area next to the shelter.

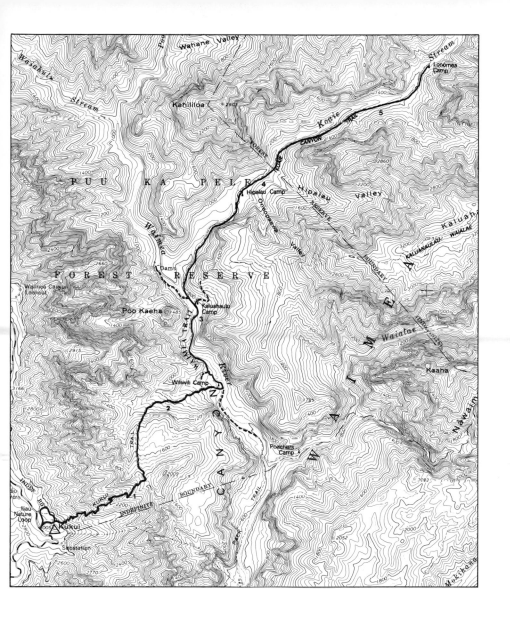

42. Alakai Swamp

2¾ hours in, 2½ hours out
1350 calories; difficulty C
3.2 miles one way
Highest point: 4040 feet
Elevation gain: 400 feet
Elevation loss: 100 feet
Map: Haena 1:24,000
Division of Forestry and Wildlife

The Alakai is the largest swamp in the Hawaiian Islands, covering about 10 square miles in the center of Kauai. In it are found some of the rarest native Hawaiian birds and plants. It has been relatively untouched by the outside world. Cattle and other livestock could not reach its interior through the deep mud, no crops could be grown, and no minerals have been found. Thus, no roads cross the area. Native birds of Hawaii have been safe from diseases spread by mosquitoes since all of the swamp is above 2,800 feet, the top limit of their range in Hawaii.

The Alakai Swamp Trail is the one relatively easy access into the swamp. Although it does not go all the way to the center of the swamp, it does lead across a portion of it, more than enough for most hikers. The Alakai Swamp is flat and featureless. As a result one can easily become lost, especially since the area is constantly cloud-covered and rainy. Assume that you will be rained upon and will be in mud above your knees. The Alakai includes areas where it rains as many as 600 inches per year. Greater than usual caution should be exercised to stay on the trail. However, route-finding is made easier by trail markers renewed annually by the Division of Forestry and Wildlife. Also, poles of a World War II telephone line parallel the trail for most of the distance. If you stray far from a well-trodden path or trail marker, it is likely that you have gone off the trail. Return to the last known point and start again. Straying is all the more likely since side trails made by hunters and wild pigs lead out periodically. In some areas there are multiple paths leading to the same loca-

Alakai Swamp

tion made by persons trying to avoid mud holes. Carry a compass.

Route: The map on page 139 shows the route along the roads to the trailhead. Start at Kokee State Park Headquarters. Check at the headquarters to see if the dirt access roads, Kumuwela andMohihi (Camp 10 Road), are passable. If the roads are not passable, use the Pihea Trail (described later) to reach the Alakai Swamp. Take Kumuwela Road, which starts 0.1 miles east of park headquarters on the south side of Highway 55. At approximately 1.3 miles the road comes to a fork. Take Mohihi Road to the left. At 3.1 miles the road reaches the forest reserve entrance sign and the Alakai Shelter picnic area. From here a side road leads 0.2 miles to the left (north) toward the Alakai Swamp, ending at a parking area.

The trail starts here and for the first mile follows the remnants of a four-wheel-drive road used for installing the World War II telephone line. Most of the poles put up at that time have been cut down. The trail passes through the first bog before it crosses the Pihea Trail in a thick stand of small

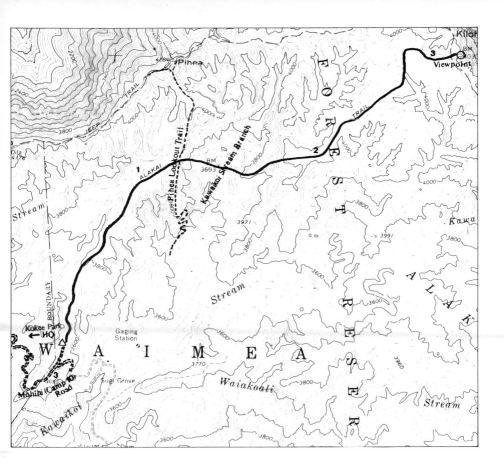

trees. Continue on deeper into the Alakai Swamp. At approximately 1.5 miles, the trail crosses a lovely branch of Kawaikoi Stream. This is a good lunch stop, a turn-around place for the less enthusiastic, and a good place to clean off the mud on your return from Kilohana.

Toward Kilohana the mud along the trail deepens. Follow the markers in the open bogs. Mist will quickly cloud camera lenses, and the air is so humid that it may be impossible to dry them off. Camera enthusiasts should take along several lens filters. About 2.5 miles from the start, the trail leaves the telephone poles for a detour about 0.2 miles to the left (north) and then quickly returns to the telephone poles and proceeds on toward the viewpoint at Kilohana.

Here you can see the Wainiha Valley below and all the way to the beaches at Hanalei, provided the weather is reasonably good. It is a spectacular sight. In spite of all the mud and difficulty in finding directions, completing the trail gives one, in retrospect, the quiet satisfaction of having been to one of the more unusual spots on earth. There is good overnight tent camping (by permit) at nearby Sugi Grove Campground and Kokee State Park. To use the cabins at Kokee State Park, be sure to make reservations well in advance.

43. Kawaikoi Stream

½ hours up, ½ hours down
500 calories; difficulty A
2.5 mile loop
Highest point: 3650 feet
Elevation gain: 50 feet
Map: Haena 1:24,000
Division of Forestry and Wildlife

This trail is located on the bank of remote and beautiful Kawaikoi Stream. It is one of the easiest and loveliest Division of Forestry and Wildlife trails on Kauai. Kawaikoi Stream is one of the principal streams draining the Alakai Swamp. It provides a habitat for many of the swamp's rare waterfowl. These may be photographed with a telephoto lens, if you approach quietly. The heavy, decaying vegetation through which the stream flows stains its waters a rich, translucent brown.

Route: The map on page 139 shows the route along the roads to the trailhead. Start at Kokee State Park Headquarters. Find out if the dirt access roads, Kumuwela and Mohihi Road (Camp 10 Road), are passable. Kumuwela Road starts 0.1 miles east of park headquarters on the south side of Highway 55. If the surface is dry, drive along Kumuwela Road approximately 1.3 miles to a fork, which may be signed "Mohihi Road" left and "Kumuwela Road" right. Keep left. At 3.7 miles from Highway 55 the dirt road reaches Kawaikoi Camp and Picnic Area and the ford across Kawaikoi Stream.

The trailhead is located 100 yards beyond the ford, on the left, across from the entrance to Sugi Grove Camp, in a dense, vigorous forest of Japanese sugi (cedar) and redwoods planted during the Great Depression. The trail leads east along the south (right) bank of Kawaikoi Stream. At about 0.7 miles a ford to the Pihea Trail leads northwest to cross the stream. The Kawaikoi Stream Trail does not cross the ford, but continues up on the south bank. At about .8 miles the trail starts a loop, with the right hand branch sidehilling east away some dis-

Blackberry

tance from the stream, returning to follow the stream atop a 40 foot bluff. The trail descends and makes a sharp left turn to a crossing near the bluff. The trail returns closely following the stream on slippery footing to a crossing to complete the loop.

Sugi Grove Campground, just a short distance along Mohihi Road, is a beautiful and seldom crowded camping area in a dense grove of large sugi trees. Since the Kawaikoi Stream Trail is only a day hike, Sugi Grove or Kokee State Campground are good spots for overnight camping in connection with hikes on this trail.

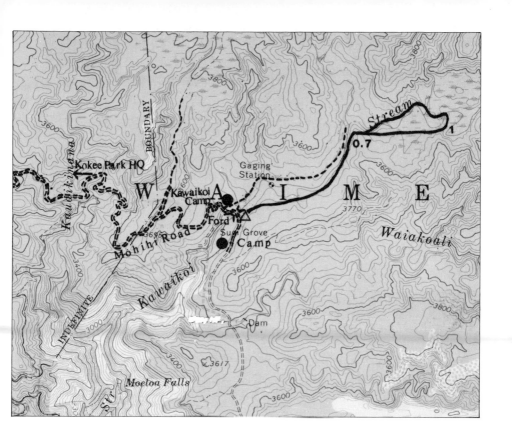

Kawaikoi Stream

44. Poomau Canyon Vista

¼ hour down, ½ hour up
175 calories; difficulty A
0.3 miles one way
Highest point: 3500 feet
Elevation loss: 100 feet
Map: Haena 1:24,000
Division of Forestry and Wildlife

Waimea Canyon is viewed by visitors in the thousands and photographed tens of thousands of times from its west side along Highway 55. While in no way deprecating the magnificent view from vantage points along its west side, there is far more to Waimea Canyon. The Kukui and Koaie Trails (described in this book) provide difficult access to the canyon floor and one of its important side canyons. For those wishing to see more of Waimea Canyon but lacking time for the longer trails, the Poomau Canyon Trail provides an additional vantage point which can be reached with a minimum of effort. The vista is an especially desirable vantage point to photograph Waimea Canyon from a new and different angle. The trail is neither so difficult nor so long that a camera enthusiast cannot haul all of his equipment down and back from the vista.

Trailhead and Norfolk Island Pine

Route: Start at Kokee State Park Headquarters. Find out if the dirt access roads, Kumuwela and Mohihi (Camp 10 Road), are passable. Kumuwela Road starts 0.1 miles east of park headquarters on the south side of Highway 55. If the surface of these dirt roads is dry, drive along Kumuwela Road approximately 1.3 miles to a fork, Mohihi Road to the left and Kumuwela Road to the right. Keep left. At 3.7 miles from Highway 55 the dirt road reaches Kawaikoi Camp and Picnic Area and then the ford across Kawaikoi Stream.

From the Kawaikoi Stream ford, the road leads past Sugi Grove Campground, a beautiful and seldom crowded campground adjacent to Kawaikoi Stream in a stand of tall Japanese sugi trees. About 0.8 miles beyond the Kawaikoi Stream crossing and shortly after the road crosses Waiakoali Stream, the

Poomau Canyon Vista Trail starts, leading off to the right from a 40-foot-high Norfolk Island Pine. The trail leads through a stand of sugi trees, across a small footbridge over an irrigation ditch paralleled by a dirt road, and then into the native upland forest. It passes a wide variety of endemic plants, then switchbacks down to the viewpoint above Poomau Canyon, where it ends. From the viewpoint you may see a great distance down the length of Poomau and Waimea canyons and watch the graceful white-tailed tropic birds gliding on the winds near the cliffs below.

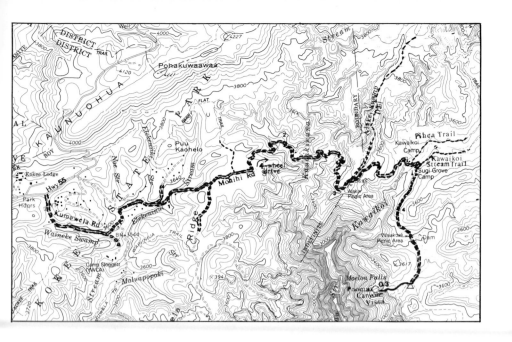

Poomau Canyon Vista

45. Awaawapuhi

1½ hours down, 2¼ hours up
1300 calories; difficulty B
3.1 miles one way
Highest point: 4100 feet
Elevation loss: 1500 feet
Maps: Haena, Makaha Point 1:24,000
Division of Forestry and Wildlife

Awesome views of the Na Pali Coast and its isolated, hanging valleys make this trail one of the best for photography in Hawaii. The trail descends 1500 feet through native dryland forests to the sheer cliffs above the remote Awaawapuhi and Nualolo Valleys. These rarely visited valleys are accessible only by water and then only after hard climbing from the sea. Yet, from the viewpoints at the end of this trail, the valleys and the great fluted walls enclosing them can be viewed from above. The sight is memorable, especially, if you sit at the viewpoints to see the sunlight and shadows play on the cliffs and sea in the late afternoon or early morning. Helicopters, flutter in and out of the steep-cliffed valleys below like dragonflies. The Division of Forestry has marked many plants along the route and has published an interpretive guide to them.

Route: The trailhead is on Highway 55, on the left, across from a dirt road, 1.6 miles toward the Kalalau Lookout from the Kokee State Park Headquarters. At first the broad trail leads north and makes a small rise. Then it descends along switchbacks, steadily northwest. It passes numbered and labelled Hawaiian plants along the way.

At 2.8 miles from the start, the connector to the Nualolo Trail leads in from the left (south). After passing this, the Awaawapuhi Trail ends at two viewpoints overlooking the great cliffs above the sea, the white-tailed tropic birds, and the inevitable 8 am helicopters. Be sure not to go close to the edges of the canyons on the eroded areas. The small stones covering the hard surfaces, like ballbearings on concrete, provide treacherous footing. The drop to the valley floor on either side is between 1500

Fluted Cliffs of the Nuololo Valley

and 2000 feet, depending on the bounce.

The native dryland forest in this area is rare and the danger of fires extreme; thus, neither overnight camping nor fires are permitted. Water is not available.

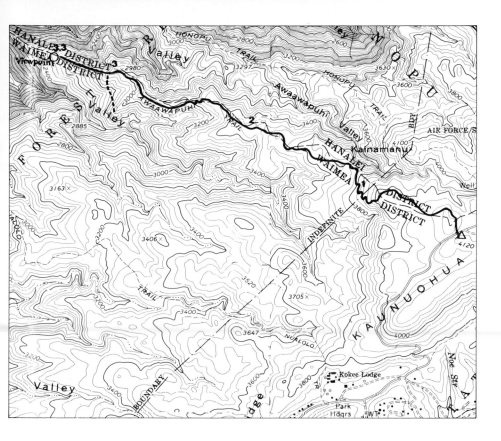

Helicopter Venturing among the Na Pali Cliffs

46. Pihea

2½ hours in, 3 hours out
1050 calories; difficulty B
3.8 miles one way
Highest point: 4284 feet
Elevation loss: 800 feet
Map: Haena 1:24,000
Division of Forestry and Wildlife

Early morning

ONLY HIKED ½ .5 MILE
ON THIS TRAIL
DRIZZLE + MIST
MUDDY & STEEP
GREAT VIEWS of NAPLI COAST
(HIKING BOOTS RECOMMENDED)

Skirting the great fluted cliffs above the Kalalau Valley, and ending along Kawaikoi Stream, the Pihea Trail provides some of the best scenery in the Hawaiian Islands. It borders the expanse of the Alakai Swamp and provides all-weather access to the Alakai Swamp Trail. The trail is most pleasant early in the morning, when you have a good chance of seeing many native Hawaiian birds feeding in the trees along the trail and goats clambering with remarkable aplomb along the precipitous cliffs below.

The ocean and sky provide an immense backdrop of varying shades of blue and white. The light of the rising sun playing on the fluted cliffs offers exceptionally good color for photos. Ohia lehua trees with their brilliant red flowers, ferns of various sorts, mosses, and white lichens are found along the trail.

Route: Take Highway 50 west from Lihue almost all the way through Waimea to Waimea Canyon Drive, beginning on the right at the Waimea Baptist Church, Follow Waimea Canyon Drive for almost 7 miles to Highway 55. Turn right onto Highway 55 and follow it past Kokee State Park, Kokee Air Force Station, and the Kalalau Lookout to the very end of the paved road at the Puu O Kila Lookout.

The trail begins at the lookout, following the remnants of a road-building attempt along the edge of the cliffs above the Kalalau Valley. Fortunately people thought better of it and work on this desecration was stopped. However, erosion started by the road cuts continues, and it is only a matter of time before the narrow ridge itself will be bisected. As the trail approaches the Alakai Swamp the vegetation becomes

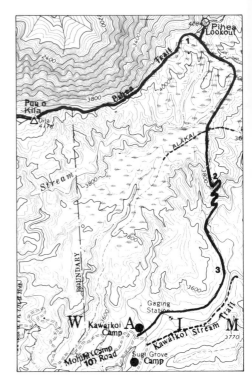

more luxuriant. After 1.1 miles a spur leads up a short distance to the Pihea Lookout.

The main trail descends southerly, skirting the bogs of the Alakai Swamp. At about 1.7 miles the trail crosses the Alakai Swamp Trail in a flat, swampy area crowded with small trees. It then makes a switchbacking descent to branches of Kawaikoi Stream. At about 3.3 miles, after crossing a small stream, the trail passes by a fair-weather ford leading across Kawaikoi Stream to the Kawaikoi Stream Trail. The Pihea Trail continues down the northwest side of Kawaikoi Stream half a mile to end at the

Pali above Kalalau Valley

Mohihi Road (Camp 10 Road).

Good overnight tent camping (by permit) is available at nearby Kokee State Park and Sugi Grove Campground. To use the cabins at Kokee State Park, make reservations well in advance.

47. Kalalau Trail

2-4 days; 9 hours in, 9 hours out
4900 calories; difficulty C
11 miles one way
Highest point: 800 feet
Elevation gain: 2000 feet
Elevation loss: 2000 feet
Map: Haena 1:24,000
Division of State Parks

Many would say that this is the best of all Hawaiian trails because of the balmy weather, massive, fluted cliffs, and the delightful, isolated beaches found along the route. The Na Pali Coast which it follows is one of the oldest portions of the Hawaiian Islands. It has been heavily eroded by the elements, forming spectacular cliffs and valleys along its entire length. The trail with modern improvements, follows the course of an ancient Hawaiian trail, parts of which are still visible.

Obtain permits for camping and for day use beyond Hanakapiai from the Division of State Parks in Lihue (open weekdays only).

Route: Take Highway 56 north to its very end, on the North Shore at Kee Beach, past Hanalei, about 38 miles from Lihue. The trail begins at a sign-in stand left of the parking lot. Several springs and streams, about an hour apart, provide treatable water along this trail. About 2 miles from the

trailhead, the trail reaches the lovely Hanakapiai Valley. At the mouth of the valley there is a sandy beach and a wilderness camping area of exceptional beauty, although in recent years it has become somewhat crowded. The Hanakapiai Falls Trail (described later), which starts where the Kalalau Trail crosses Hanakapiai Stream, leads to the falls in this valley. From Hanakapiai Stream, the Kalalau Trail climbs steeply, crossing the Hoolulu and Waiahuakua Valleys before reaching the Hanakoa Valley, midway on the trail. In summer,

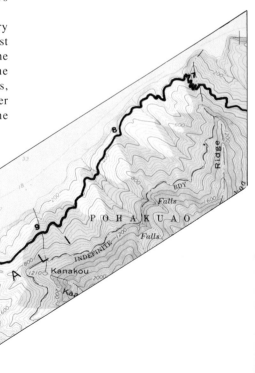

guava and mountain apple are plentiful along this trail. There is much evidence of taro cultivation in earlier times.

At 6.0 miles, the trail reaches Hanakoa Shack, a shelter available to hikers. Camping sites are located nearby and water is plentiful. A short path leads from the front of the shelter to Hanakoa Pool, a delightful swimming hole in Hanakoa Stream. Just beyond the stream, a short side trail, called the Hanakoa Falls Trail (described later), leads upstream to the falls.

The Na Pali Coast

About 9.5 miles from the start, the trail begins to descend the east slope of the Kalalau Valley to the beach, past numerous stone walls and former taro patches. The last of these patches was abandoned by the twenties.

Proceed along one of the paths paralleling the beach. The permitted camping area is just inland, toward the west end of the beach. Treatable water is available from the cascading part of a small waterfall located at the west end of the beach.

Strong currents along the Na Pali Coast have caused drownings. In places this long trail can be frighteningly narrow and exposed or slippery when wet. Nonetheless, even a short hike to the first viewpoints is rewarding. The hike all the way to Kalalau Beach and back is incomparable.

48. Hanakapiai Falls
via 47. Kalalau Trail
3¼ hours in, 3 hours out
1500 calories; difficulty B
3.8 miles one way
Highest point: 800 feet
Elevation gain: 1150 feet
Elevation loss: 400 feet
Map: Haena 1:24,000
Division of State Parks

This lovely trail leads into a sheltered valley, once thickly settled. Now only scattered, abandoned taro patches, stone walls, and house foundations remain as evidence of the once-thriving agricultural population. From ancient times the fertility of the soil and the abundance of water made the valley well suited for taro production. Later, cash crops were raised. However, since the area was small and far from the markets, such enterprises proved unprofitable. The trail passes the ruins of a small coffee mill which used Hanakapiai Stream as its power source. Little remains except a large stone chimney.

Cattle raising was attempted after the people left the valley, but this proved so destructive to the land that the cattle were finally removed and the land was placed under state administration. In this status it has been gradually recovering for the last four decades. The scattered descendants of the various cultivated plants now richly cover the valley floor. An occasional taro plant grows haphazardly next to kukui trees. Guava and mango offer their succulent fruit to passersby, and the worst of man's abuses are slowly being erased.

Route: The Hanakapiai Falls Trail branches off the Kalalau Trail. To reach the Kalalau Trail, follow the directions under that heading. The head of the Hanakapiai Valley Trail is marked by a large sign about 2 miles from the beginning of the Kalalau Trail and shortly after it crosses Hanakapiai Stream. The trail leads up the west bank of Hanakapiai Stream and is fairly easy for about a mile. It passes close by the coffee mill ruins toward the beginning of the trail. Further on, the route becomes increasingly

Monstera

difficult and crosses to the other side of the stream.

The trail leads by a series of lovely, small waterfalls and pools and ultimately ends at the main waterfall. There, a broad, deep pool formed by the falls provides ample room for a refreshing swim. Large stones surrounding the pool make fine perches for sunbathing.

Crossing points and the trail itself are subject to change because of changes in the stream and use of the trail. The trail is not well defined at this time. However, if you follow the main stream, you will not go far wrong. If the stream is flooding, it is best not to continue since the upper crossings become progressively more difficult. When swimming in the pool below the main falls, beware of rocks swept down in the falls, especially during high water. Camping is permitted near Hanakapiai Beach. Permits

Hanakapiai Beach

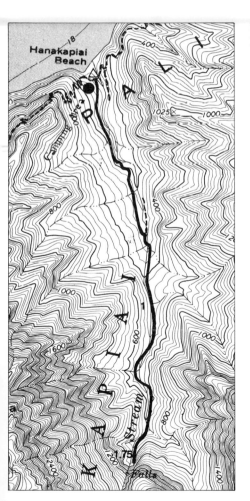

must be obtained during weekday working hours at the Division of State Parks in Lihue. Strong currents may make the beach unsafe for swimming.

147

49. Hanokoa
via 47. Kalalau Trail
1-2 days; 5 hours in, 5 hours out
2400 calories; difficulty B
6.5 miles one way
Highest point: 800 feet
Elevation gain: 1600 feet
Elevation loss: 800 feet
Haena 1:24,000
Division of State Parks

This short extension off the Kalalau Trail leads to a waterfall and pool much like that on the Hanakapiai Falls Trail described earlier. It has the additional attraction of being even farther off the beaten path. This side trail is short, but since it is farther along the Kalalau Trail, most people are too weary to take it to the lovely pool at its end.

Route: The trail begins near the 6.0 mile mark on the Kalalau Trail, just beyond Hanakoa Shack and about 20 yards west of the crossing of Hanakoa Stream. To reach the Kalalau Trail trailhead, see the description in this book under that trail.

The Hanakoa Falls Trail first traverses the remnants of taro terraces close to the Kalalau Trail, then crosses the west fork of Hanakoa Stream. Keep low on the far bank at the crossing and go downstream for a few yards. The trail will shortly become apparent as it leads away from the west fork to continue along the steep west bank of the east fork of Hanakoa Stream. On the way it passes above several small pools and waterfalls where slides may make the trail too hazardous to attempt. It finally reaches the large pool below Hanakoa Falls.

There, deliciously cool water cascades from the Alakai Swamp, 3,000 feet above, into the pool. A swim is especially enjoyable after the long hike down the Kalalau Trail. The deep, wide pool is surrounded by high cliffs on three sides, with a second waterfall to the east which cascades only during wet weather. These cliffs seem to be a favorite haunt of the white-tailed tropic bird, a swallow-like bird with a strange habit of flying full speed toward cliffs and veering to safety inches before impact. To lie in the warm sun after a long

Cool water

hike and a cool swim, looking up at these graceful white birds playing near the waterfall and cliffs, is one of life's better pastimes.

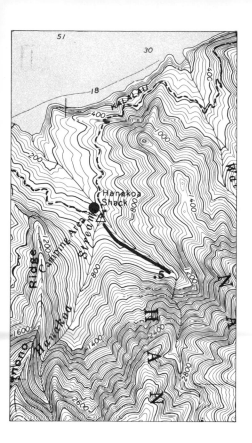

Hanakoa Falls

And this our life exempt from public
  haunt
Finds tongues in trees, books in the
  running brooks,
Sermons in stones, and good in
  everything.
I would not change it.

Shakespeare, *As You Like It,* II, i